AN INTRODUCTION TO TACITUS

AN INTRODUCTION TO TACITUS

HERBERT W. BENARIO

UNIVERSITY OF GEORGIA PRESS
ATHENS

Library of Congress Catalog Card Number: 73–85025
ISBN: 0–8203–0328–3 (cloth); 0–8203–0361–5 (paper)

The University of Georgia Press, Athens 30602

Copyright © 1975 by the University of Georgia Press
Printed in the United States of America

MANIBVS MATRIS CARISSIMAE
PATRI OPTIMO
VXORI DVLCISSIMAE
QVI OMNES ALIVS ALITER
TOT ANNOS ADIVVERINT
DEDICAT AVCTOR

PREFACE

There have been many books and articles on Tacitus in the years since the end of World War II. The output has been so steady that some scholars ask plaintively in reviews, "Is another book on Tacitus necessary?" That I have undertaken to write another shows my conviction that at least one more is indeed necessary, and my hope is that the present volume will meet the purpose which I envisage for it.

The availability of many books does not mean that all potential audiences are equally satisfied and their needs met. In the course of my own teaching, I have become increasingly aware that there is no single volume, reasonable in compass, up-to-date, and reliable, to which I could direct my students who were meeting Tacitus for the first or second time and who were not ready for the greater works in the field to which all Taciteans are indebted. I hope that this gap will now be filled. This book is not intended to be pretentious; I have drawn upon the views of many scholars in synthesizing my own judgments, but there is also much which will, perhaps, attract the attention of these same scholars. Sir Ronald Syme's great and massive *Tacitus* lies behind this volume, as it does behind almost everything written in the field, but the novice cannot digest it with ease. Other books, because of their different focus or imprecision, have not been altogether suitable for the needs of the less advanced reader.

The English translations for the minor works are taken from my own publication (Bobbs–Merrill 1967), for the *Annals* from A. J. Church and W. J. Brodribb's *The Annals of Tacitus* (Macmillan 1906), for the *Histories* from their companion volume *The History of Tacitus* (Macmillan 1872), for Sallust from S. A. Handford's *Sallust: Jugurthine War* and *Conspiracy of Catiline* (Penguin 1963), for Pliny's *Letters* and *Panegyricus* from B. Radice's edition in the Loeb Library (Harvard and Heinemann 1969), for the speech of the Emperor Claudius on the admission of Gauls to the Senate from A. C. Johnson, P. R. Coleman-Norton, and F. C. Bourne, *Ancient Roman Statutes* (Texas 1961). I am grateful to Bobbs–Merrill, Penguin, Harvard, Heinemann, and Texas for permission to reproduce the translations that they published. I also wish to thank the editors of *American Journal of Philology, Classical World*, and *Classical Journal* for permission to reuse material in articles of mine that first appeared in their pages, and the authorities of Bobbs–Merrill once again for permission to use part of the introduction to my translation of *Tacitus: Agricola, Germany, Dialogue on Orators*.

I have profited from the comments and criticisms of Sir Ronald Syme, Miss Norma P. Miller, and Professor Glen W. Bowersock and thank them once again for their courtesy and generosity; any shortcomings that may remain are my sole responsibility. My wife has, as always, been a part of this work from the very beginning; without her encouragement and support I could have accomplished very little. Mrs. Jacqueline Alexander has typed the manuscript thrice, from roughest version to final draft. Her skill in decipherment and her pains-taking care have put me greatly in her debt.

The absence of footnotes is intentional, to promote ease and rapidity of reading. Essential references, largely citations of classical literature, have been inserted into the text. The scholar will easily recognize from the text itself the modern authors to whom I am most beholden, the student will gain guidance through the vast field of Tacitean studies from the Selected Bibliography at the end.

Publication of this book was assisted by the Emory University Research Committee through a grant and by the American Council of Learned Societies under a grant from the Andrew W. Mellon Foundation. In addition, I wish to thank Dr. Wolfgang Oberleitner, Curator of Antiquities, Kunsthistorisches Museum, Vienna, for permission to reproduce a photograph of the Museum's Eagle cameo, dated about 40 A.D., on the book cover and the dust jacket.

TABLE OF CONTENTS

I. HISTORICAL BACKGROUND

Tacitus's life spanned the first and second centuries of our era. His subjects were men and events of the Roman Empire; only rarely does he, in the course of his narrative, go back, beyond his self-imposed starting point, to the earlier days of the republic. Nonetheless, although his historical work is localized in time and place, it has an import and meaning far more general and universal, which cannot be understood without the backdrop of all Roman history. The historical background for Tacitus's age and writings thus begins not with the establishment of the empire but with the very foundation of Rome itself.

It is well enough known that, as tradition recorded, Rome was founded by Romulus in the middle of the eighth century B.C. The monarchy survived for approximately two and one-half centuries until Tarquinius Superbus was expelled because of private vices and public crimes and the republic established under the prime impetus of Lucius Junius Brutus. The king was removed, but his powers were not destroyed. He was succeeded by two magistrates, the consuls, whose *imperium* was as unlimited in scope as it was in effect. But the consuls had limitations placed upon their power that the king had not had, since their terms were limited to one year and each could veto the action of the other. The government of the Roman Republic is marked above all by the magistracy, of which the consulate is the chief but not the only one. It was this executive which gave the Roman State the ability to react to crises and to meet them boldly with proper leadership. It was, however, rather the body of accumulated wisdom, the Senate, into which all ex-consuls passed after they had completed their term of office, and of which other magistrates were members as well, which gave Rome the stability and the continuity that enabled her to become the greatest power in the Mediterranean world.

For about two hundred years Rome struggled with internal crises; as was not uncommon in antiquity, the people were divided between the land owners and those dependent upon them. The political control of the state was, at first, completely in the hands of the patricians, the aristocracy by birth; as time passed, members of the plebeian class whose economic and social status demanded recognition won a share in the control of political office. This period, known as the Struggle of the Orders, gradually opened up all offices of the state to the plebeian class, with the result that a new aristocracy, not of birth but of office, developed.

This aristocracy justly claimed credit for Rome's survival in the greatest challenge to her existence that she ever faced, the second Punic War when Hannibal brought her to her knees but was unable to crush her, and then guided her during the subsequent period of expansion over the major part of the Mediterranean basin. During this great war, in the year 216, Rome suffered a disaster in battle at Cannae which surpassed any that had up to that point befallen her and which, at least emotionally, was greater than any that she was to receive in the centuries that followed. Hannibal, a genius in generalship, had invaded Italy after a surprise and superb expedition across southern France and through the Alps, had won two small battles, and then had inflicted a major defeat upon the Romans at Lake Trasimene the year before Cannae. He did not, after Trasimene, march upon Rome, but crossed the Apennines into Apulia, the southeastern part of the Italian peninsula, and there was met by both Roman consuls with an army of some eighty thousand men. In one of the classic battles of all history, one which is still considered a model by students of military tactics, Hannibal destroyed this army to such a degree that Rome was brought closer to lasting defeat than she ever had been brought before. The public treasury was exhausted, manpower was no longer readily available, the city of Rome itself lay open to attack. It was at this point in his narrative of Rome's rise in the Mediterranean world from the beginning of the first Punic War that Polybius, a Greek historian, paused to ask the important question of why Rome did not collapse. There was no instance known to him in all history when a city or state had suffered such a critical disaster and had continued, not only to fight, but ultimately to triumph. What was it that gave Rome the ability to recover and then win?

He answered his own question by an examination of the Roman constitution. In a famous discussion he discerned that Rome was singularly free of that disease of the body politic from which Greek city-states had suffered, seemingly from time immemorial. This was *stasis*, political upheaval, lack of stability, which brought cyclical changes without prospects for improvement in government for the future. Perhaps the most important discussion of *stasis* in antiquity is that of Thucydides, in the *Peloponnesian War*, III:82–83, where he penetratingly examines the Corcyrean revolt. *Stasis* in Greek city-states developed because one element of society was violently opposed to another for social, economic, and political reasons. This led, in due course, to revolt. The defeated party was driven out only to return, in time, to gain the upper hand, and to impose similar penalties upon its opponents.

This had not happened at Rome. Polybius claimed that the reason for this fact was that the various levels of society at Rome were not opposed to each other but worked in alliance with each other. This was the case because Rome could not be designated an aristocracy or a democracy or a monarchy, but rather was a mixed constitution embracing all three pure forms of government. The magistrates represented the monarchical element, the Senate the aristocratic, and the people in their assemblies the democratic. Each of the three had important powers and rights which could not be transgressed and without which the state could not function properly. There was, consequently, not rivalry but cooperation and, at the great moments of crises, a belief among all Roman citizens that it was their survival that was at stake rather than the supremacy of one group over another.

Polybius's analysis, although it may be wrong in detail and does not give sufficient importance to the overwhelmingly oligarchic nature of the Roman state through the significance of the Senate, is nonetheless, in the last analysis, basically true. It can be seen, from this point on, how all Romans pulled together until, with the passage of another decade and a half, Hannibal had not only left Italy but had been defeated in his homeland, and then how, in the half-century that followed, Rome was able to become the mistress of much of the Mediterranean world.

The years 220 to 168, the period which was Polybius's prime concern in the first version of his history, were those that represented the heyday of the Senate. One cannot say that the Senate comported itself properly at all times; but it did, nonetheless, represent what Pyrrhus's ambassadors, early in the third century, had spoken of as an assembly of kings. However, with the expansion of Rome, the influx of wealth from the newly won provinces brought about a significant change in the character of the Roman ruling class. There no longer was the scrupulous integrity that had made a Roman's word his bond; Polybius had been moved to say that, when a Roman gave his word, it was worth more than all the oaths of the Greeks. The third Punic War was invoked by Rome, perhaps in fear of Carthage's rising military power, perhaps even more in jealousy of her economic prowess. Whatever the reason, Carthage was destroyed in 146 and, from that point on, Rome had no rival.

It was, for the historian Sallust, a most crucial year. In his monographs Sallust probed the breakdown of Roman honor and Roman stability. His answer to the queries of why and when this occurred focused precisely upon the year 146 because the *metus hostilis*, the fear of an enemy, was eliminated with the destruction of Carthage. This too is an oversimplification because there were instances, alas too numerous, of Roman moral breakdown before 146. But the year, nonetheless, represents a watershed. Henceforth the prime goal of many Roman senators is not the well-being of the state nor, and it might be said that this is even more important, the well-being of the provincials, but their own aggrandizement, so that instances of plunder and extortion become so numerous that they are a scandal in the annals of the late republic.

Along with this external change, there develops a rivalry within the state between members of the ruling class known as the nobility. *Nobilitas*, in Roman political language, means that a man comes from a family which has at some time had a consulate. The nobility were the most important members of the senatorial order; their numbers were quite small, perhaps no more than two dozen great families. As wealth from the provinces, particularly from the Greek East, poured into Rome, those who benefited most immediately were the upper class. The influx of money and of bullion raised prices, thereby lowering the standard of living of the great mass of the populace. Further, constant warfare had caused many citizens to lose their land and to flock to Rome.

In the year 133 Tiberius Sempronius Gracchus entered upon the office of tribune. His nobility was as high as that of any young man in the Roman state. He was the son of the similarly named Tiberius Sempronius Gracchus, perhaps the leading figure of the plebeian nobility, who had twice held the consulate and had been censor. His mother Cornelia was the daughter of the great Publius Cornelius Scipio Africanus who had defeated Hannibal in the year 202. A normal public career, culminating in a consulship, unquestionably awaited Tiberius. But he chose rather to attack the internal ills of the state. His experience in Spain in the early 130's and his own understanding of the malaise of Italy led him to break sharply with the ruling aristocracy. His prime purpose was to redistribute land and to get many of the poor who now lived in Rome back on the soil, thereby reconstituting the strong and vigorous peasant class that had served as the basis of Rome's armies for so long and had been the bulwark of her political stability.

Whether because of personal arrogance or an unwillingness to compromise, Tiberius alienated those whose support he desperately needed until a complete break was inevitable. His laws were passed but, toward the end of his term of office, he was assassinated. Not only was this an act against the gods, since the sacrosanctity of a tribune had now been violated, but it was in a way even more portentous because it was the first instance of the shedding of Roman blood by a Roman in considerably more than three centuries. It boded ill and ill was quick to come.

Tiberius's brother Gaius continued but expanded his program in his own tribunate in 123–122, thereby making irrevocable the split between what now began to be called the *populares* and the *optimates*. In the years since Tiberius's murder violence had become an accepted way of life in Rome's dealings not only with foreign peoples but with her allies in Italy and with dissident members of the aristocracy in the capital itself. Since that was the case, it did not take long before a challenge came against an aristocracy now generally charged with incompetence, unscrupulousness, dishonesty, and self-seeking, a challenge spearheaded by a champion who not only represented a cause but also mustered armed might which proved to be a personal army.

This champion was Marius; aged forty-nine, he had not yet held the consulate and was given small hope of holding one until he would be too old to pursue a public career of any significance beyond it. He chose not to remain quiet but to challenge the greatest family of the *optimates*, the Metelli. Not only did he succeed to an important military command, but he was subsequently elected to five successive consulates, a distinction that no man in Rome's history had been able to claim. The army proved the key to his personal advancement.

What one had done, others clearly could do as well. Marius, in his turn, was challenged by a former lieutenant, Sulla, a more penetrating and able political figure who, at the end of his civil war against the aristocracy dominated by the *populares*, re-established the primacy of the *optimates* with himself as dictator for some three years. Sulla was supported in his cause by a young man named Gnaeus Pompeius, who, in his early twenties, raised an army at his own expense and put it at Sulla's disposal, and then was able to challenge his master. The constitution which Sulla had so painstakingly put together in an attempt to restore the primacy of the senatorial order was dismantled bit by bit under the leadership of Pompey, who became known as *Magnus*, "The Great." The decades of the seventies and the sixties are the decades of Pompey's primacy, a period when this man who had held no public office before the consulate, which he extorted from the Senate when he was still well below the legal age, was honored with a series of extraordinary commands. His reputation late in the sixties was unparalleled, and perhaps greater than that of any man since the days of the Scipios. His great rival was a man of eminent background and extraordinary talent, Gaius Julius Caesar.

Julius Caesar, a far shrewder statesman and politician than Pompey, and at the least his match militarily, was the dominant figure of the fifties with his command in Gaul, his conquest of that large and important land, and his distant influence on the political scene in Rome. Pompey could not brook a rival, much less a superior, and by the end of the fifties he had become the champion of the senatorial order, the *optimates*, that group of men whose power he above all had shaken. Civil war seemed inevitable, and so indeed it proved. Caesar and Pompey met on the battlefield at Pharsalus in the year 48, with Caesar victorious. Pompey fled to Egypt and was put to death by the ministers of Ptolemy as he landed. For the next several years Caesar undertook to wipe out the remnants of Pompey's forces until, without a rival, dictator for life and consul, he dominated all; men of republican leanings, jealous that one of their peers should now be their master, undertook to remove this cancer from the fabric of the state and, on the famous Ides of March, forty-four, assassinated him.

Nothing was accomplished by this. Caesar was gone but Caesarism remained. The surviving consul, Antony, seized the reins of state, and the liberators, led by Brutus and Cassius, were dumbfounded to realize that the populace did not look upon them as heroes. Had there been no individuals of current political import other than Antony, Brutus, and Cassius, some *modus vivendi* might well have been established. But Caesar in his will had adopted his grandnephew, a young man of frail health, then eighteen years old, named Gaius Octavius. By this posthumous adoption, the young Octavius received the name of Gaius Julius Caesar Octavianus and, after some moments of indecision, against the advice of most of his friends and family, decided to come to Rome to claim his inheritance.

Antony chose first to ignore him and to do him out of this inheritance, counting upon his prestige as the head of Caesar's supporters, for he had been Caesar's prime associate and chief military lieutenant. His miscalculation was great, for the young man was the new Caesar in more than merely name.

As it turned out, with the turmoil of civil war only so recently ended, more civil war was to come. At first, Antony and Octavian were on opposing sides, but Octavian was no natural ally of the senatorial order now championed by Cicero, an order which had been responsible for and had rejoiced in the murder of his adoptive father. Politics do make strange bedfellows; yet, in the long run, mutual interests tend to prevail, and so it happened in the year 43. Antony and Octavian joined Lepidus to form officially the second triumvirate and thereby they became the masters of the Roman state; they first undertook to eliminate their enemies by proscription not only to satisfy personal enmities but also to gain the money required for their armies by confiscation of property and then to destroy the forces of the "liberators" in armed conflict.

In 42 at Philippi, in two battles three weeks apart, the forces of Antony and Octavian were successful. It may be, with the deaths of Brutus and Cassius, that the republic can be said to have come to an end for, as Shakespeare said of Cassius, he was "The last of all the Romans," and of Brutus, "This was the noblest Roman of them all." There were now no rivals to the triumvirate. The only rivalry that existed was among the three. One of them, Lepidus, can be easily discounted. He was inferior in prestige and personal ability and was from the beginning the junior partner. The decade of the thirties led inevitably to the final clash between Antony and Octavian. We need not go into the details nor rehearse the charges, true or not, of Antony's relationship with Cleopatra, nor need we review Octavian's skillful mobilizing of public opinion against Antony until he was finally recognized as the champion of Italy and the western provinces against the scourge of the East.

On September 2, 31, one of the most momentous battles in the history of the world was fought at Actium. Octavian's forces were victorious; Antony and Cleopatra fled to Egypt where the following year they committed suicide. But this was not important. The crucial thing was that, after Actium, the Roman world had only one master. Octavian controlled some sixty legions and nine hundred warships, and there was no one to challenge him. The question uppermost in the minds of all people in Italy and elsewhere was, "What would Octavian do now that he was alone?" He had attained the position that his father Caesar had had, but Caesar had rivals in the representatives of the ruling class who remembered when he was no more than one of them. These did not survive in sufficient number to cause Octavian concern, and there was none who could muster an army against him. In past years the return of a triumphant general from the east had been the cause of dread and trepidation. When Sulla had returned in the late eighties, civil war had come and been followed by a dictatorship. Pompey, twenty years later, had disbanded his army when he landed at Brundisium and then found that he had misplayed his cards. Soon thereafter, in order to gain his due, he was driven into the arms of Caesar in that unofficial alliance known as the first triumvirate. What course would Octavian follow?

Octavian was by nature a conservative. He chose not to follow Caesar in using the title of dictator or perhaps aspiring to kingship, but rather, in the first years after Actium, undertook to re-establish the constitutional framework of the republic without, however, relinquishing the control over the military and the finances of the empire that he had in his hands. The republic was indeed restored, *respublica restituta*, but his own position was paramount in the state. Octavian had perhaps received impetus for such a settlement from Cicero, for the principate represented the kind of government that Cicero had yearned for in his essay *De republica* (*On the Commonwealth*) where he described the best form of government as that which existed in Rome but which had added to the existing constitution a man both above the regular magistrates and apart from them as a guiding spirit, the *gubernator*, the *rector*, the *moderator*, the *tutor* or (Cicero may have used the word in a part of the work now lost) the *princeps*. Augustus (he was given this title in 27) was the *princeps*. All republican offices continued to exist; the Senate had considerable authority but, nonetheless, Augustus controlled the provinces which had almost all the military garrisons and he received the revenues of those provinces. In addition he was the great patron of all the people in the empire. Indeed, in 2 B.C. he was recognized as "father of his country."

The principate was an experiment. There had been numbers of experiments in Rome's history when one man or another had been supreme and yet, when that man died, the situation changed and generally reverted to what had existed before, senatorial control of government. There was no guarantee that the same thing would not happen to the principate when Augustus died. But Augustus, frail as he had been in his youth, outlived most of his peers. From the battle of Actium until his death is a span of almost forty-five years. There were very few left who had seen the free republic, very few who had seen Caesar, and not too many who were of an age of reason in the year of Actium. The principate that Augustus evolved by trial and error, compromise and addition, over a period of some twenty-five years from the first settlement, as it is called, in 28 and 27, had become a way of life to most of the Roman world. With minor exceptions it had brought peace, prosperity, and security to individuals, good government at home and in the provinces. There was no reason for very many to yearn for a return to the turmoil of the late republic, a period when there was no law, no order, and no respect for custom.

When Augustus died, it was perhaps inevitable that he should be succeeded by the man whom he had designated as his logical successor, after the death of earlier choices, his stepson, Tiberius. Tiberius reigned twenty-three years and was succeeded by Gaius, known as Caligula, whose reign was cut short by assassination after four years. There then followed Claudius and Nero for a span of twenty-seven years until the latter's murder brought the Julio-Claudian dynasty to an end; the year of the four emperors, as it is called, saw Galba, Otho, and Vitellius reign briefly, until Vespasian won the day and was able to establish a dynasty. The Flavian dynasty, with Vespasian succeeded by his sons Titus and Domitian, survived for twenty-seven years until Domitian was assassinated and was succeeded by a man chosen by the Senate from its own number, the elderly Nerva.

Nerva, however, was too old, too weak, too much the civilian to count upon a peaceful reign without the support of the man recognized as Rome's leading general, Trajan. Trajan was adopted and, within a year, succeeded to the purple at the death of Nerva. Trajan entered upon office with a great reputation not only as a soldier but as an individual and administrator; very early in his reign he began to be known as the *optimus princeps*, the best of emperors.

It was during the reigns of Trajan and his successor Hadrian that the mature Tacitus wrote. Tacitus saw and participated in much of the political activity of the second half of the first century A.D., and all that of the reign of Trajan. Yet his experience as a political figure in these years is perhaps no more important than the emotional impact which came to him from his reading and from his thinking about the principate of the age of Augustus. Tacitus never knew anything other than the principate; nonetheless, it may be that he was not fully willing to accept that which he knew must be. In his case, as with most Roman historians, it is politics that make the historian.

II. THE MAN
AND HIS MILIEU

Only a few details of Tacitus's life are known. At the beginning of the *Histories* (1:1,3) he tells us that his *dignitas*, his status as a member of the senatorial order, began under Vespasian, increased under Titus, and was further advanced under Domitian. In a chapter of the *Annals* (XI:11,1), he tells us that he was both praetor and a member of the college of the *quindecimviri sacris faciundis*, that body of priests who had charge of the Sibylline books and many of the special festivals of the Roman state. At this time in particular, the year 88, since the secular games were being celebrated by Domitian, it was a college of the utmost importance.

From these details, one can reconstruct his earlier career. Knowledge of an individual's progress and advancement through the *cursus honorum* in the early empire makes it possible to infer that Tacitus was born soon after the beginning of Nero's principate in the years 55 to 57. Of his ancestry, we know nothing for certain. It may be that his birthplace was in Gallia Narbonensis or, perhaps, Cisalpine Gaul. It is quite probable that he was not a Roman born in Rome, nor is it likely that he was a member of the old Roman aristocracy. Pliny the Elder records (*NH* VII:76) an imperial procurator, financial officer of Gallia Belgica, named Cornelius Tacitus.

The name is sufficiently uncommon to render it likely that this man is the historian's father.

Tacitus's career began with the customary minor offices leading to the first post of the regular *cursus*, the quaestorship. These lesser magistracies were held under Vespasian; we do not know the years of office nor the precise posts he filled but, obviously, he must have done well enough to have made the acquaintance of some of the foremost men of the state and to have attracted the attention of the rising Agricola, who had served with distinction as a legionary commander in Britain, had been chosen by Vespasian to be governor of Aquitania and, in the year 77, held the consulate. In that year Agricola gave his daughter to Tacitus in marriage, shortly before he himself went off to govern Britain for the lengthy span of seven years.

Tacitus's quaestorship followed in 81 or 82. Whether he filled the office in the last year of Titus's brief reign or the first full year of Domitian's is inconsequential. Clearly he will have been designated by Titus, and thereby the favor of that emperor for him was openly shown. In 88, as mentioned above, he was praetor and then, for a period of four years, he was away from Rome, most likely as a legionary commander under a consular governor. We know nothing more about his absence; near the end of this absence his father-in-law died (*Agr.* 45,5). When he returned to Rome, his career was obviously not stalled by the reign of terror and the crushing of the morale of the senatorial order, which both he and Pliny the Younger detailed in their writings.

In 96, Domitian was murdered. The Senate chose his successor. He was an elderly member of their own body, Marcus Cocceius Nerva. For the first time since the beginning of the principate, the Senate had been able to impose its choice upon the armies and the praetorian guard. This success, however, was relatively short lived, for the praetorian guard, resenting the death of Domitian, who had shown them great favor, rose in opposition and, in the latter part of 97, the impending crisis of government was settled by the decision that Marcus Ulpius Traianus, commander of the legions in Upper Germany, should be chosen as Nerva's adopted son and designated successor. The decision to adlect Trajan to the purple was presumably taken by a council in conjunction with Nerva. We can infer from the available evidence that Tacitus was suffect consul late in that year, and it may well be that he participated in the deliberations that brought Trajan to the fore.

His consular year was marked by only one other event of importance, the funeral oration which he delivered at the obsequies of the great Verginius Rufus, who could have claimed the purple after the murder of Nero had he not preferred to leave the choice to the Senate. His epitaph was appropriate (Pliny the Younger, *Ep.*, VI:10,4; IX:19,1):

> *Hic situs est Rufus, pulso qui Vindice quondam*
> *imperium adseruit, non sibi sed patriae.*
>
> Here lies Rufus, who once defeated Vindex
>   and set free the imperial power
> Not for himself, but for his country.

The next event of which we know in Tacitus's public career is his joint prosecution with Pliny of Marius Priscus, former governor of Africa, who was charged by the provincials with extortion. The case was won, and Tacitus spoke, as Pliny put it, with majesty, thereby confirming his reputation as perhaps the leading orator of his day. Then for a dozen years we know nothing. We do not know whether, after the year 100, he went away to a province again or performed some other public function, or whether he devoted himself entirely to the writing of history. In the year 112–113 he was, on epigraphical evidence, governor of the province of Asia. This was the culmination of a senatorial career. The provinces of Asia and Africa were the two jewels in the administrative *cursus* under senatorial control. A man of distinction and worth could hope that, at a time some fifteen years after his consulate, he would be tapped for one of these two provinces. When Tacitus returned to Rome, he again devoted himself totally to history; he probably died early in the principate of Hadrian, although this is by no means certain.

This outline of Tacitus's career is sketchy; yet, in comparison with the careers of many eminent men, both in the republic and in the empire, we know a great deal. We have the outline of an outstandingly successful political career which testified to the continuing favor of successive emperors, but this bare outline is made much fuller by the often tedious loquaciousness of his friend, Pliny the Younger.

Pliny's career paralleled that of Tacitus. He was some five years younger, came from Comum in Cisalpine Gaul, reached the quaestorship late in the eighties, the praetorship probably in 93, and the consulate in 100. On the occasion of his entry into that office on September 1, he delivered a long address of gratitude to Trajan, the text of which, in expanded form, survives: the famous *Panegyricus*. It gives us an example of the kind of oratory which had now become popular and vital in the late first and early second centuries A.D.

Pliny's career after his consulate embraced several offices, including a curatorship at Rome and finally, in the years 111– 113 (it may be that these dates are one or two years too late), a period almost contemporary with Tacitus's service in Asia, he was sent by Trajan to Bithynia to straighten out the snarl of that province's political and financial troubles. He perhaps died there.

Pliny was a prolific letter writer. Unlike Cicero, his model and master, who did not anticipate that his own correspondence would ever be published, Pliny wrote with an eye to posterity, and we have more than a dozen letters either addressed to Tacitus or addressed to others giving information about Tacitus. These enable us to put a good deal of flesh and muscle on the skeleton of the man and his career that we have already sketched.

The letters fall into three general groups; we may designate them friendly exchanges of a general nature, those dealing with history and literature, and those which are biographical. The first group is the largest, consisting of seven letters; the others comprise four letters each.

In 1:6, Pliny writes Tacitus that, on one occasion when he went hunting, he took his writing materials with him so that if he did not have any success at the hunt, he at least would not have wasted his time completely. And he urges Tacitus the next time he goes hunting also to take his notebook along with his food and drink.

In IV:13, also addressed to Tacitus, Pliny's salutation is "I am glad to hear of your safe arrival in Rome." It may be, since the letter is written about four years after the trial of Priscus, that Tacitus had been away in a province, perhaps as governor. It need not be; it may only refer to the fact that he has been off in the country and now, late in the year, he has returned to Rome. Pliny tells in this letter of an occasion not long ago when he was back in Comum, when he was amazed to learn that the young men of the town had to go away for their education since there was no appropriate school in the community. He therefore proposed that the fathers of the city collect a sum of money with which to hire teachers, and he himself offered to match a third of whatever they would be able to accrue. Pliny then asks Tacitus to be on the lookout among his followers for potential teachers, for there were many who were attracted to Tacitus by their admiration for his talent, *ex admiratione ingenii tui.*

The next letter, VI:9, is very brief. Tacitus had recommended a mutual friend who was a candidate for public office to Pliny to secure his support, and Pliny replies that this is unnecessary; yet he himself would have done the same if he, Pliny, had been away from Rome while Tacitus was in the capital. Clearly we know from this letter that Tacitus was currently absent from Rome, though we do not know where.

In letter VII:20, a relatively brief exposition of the joys of friendship and the harmony that prevails between the two men, Pliny tells of the pleasure he obtains from their relation. It merits quotation in full.

> I have read your book, and marked as carefully as I could the passages which I think should be altered or removed, for if it is my custom to tell the truth, you are always willing to hear it; no one accepts criticism so readily as those who best deserve praise. Now I am awaiting the return of my book from you, with your comments: a fair exchange which we both enjoy. I am delighted to think that if posterity takes any interest in us the tale will everywhere be told of the harmony, frankness, and loyalty of our lifelong relationship. It will seem both rare and remarkable that two men of much the same age and position, and both enjoying a certain amount of literary reputation (I can't say much about you

when it refers to me too), should have encouraged each other's literary work.

I was still a young man when you were already winning fame and glory, and I aspired to follow in your footsteps and be "far behind but still the nearest" to you in fact and in repute. There were at the time many other distinguished men of talent, but a certain similarity in our natures made me feel that you were the person I could and should try to imitate. So I am all the happier to know that whenever conversation turns upon literature, our names are mentioned together, and that my name comes up when people talk about you. There may be writers who are ranked higher than either of us, but if we are classed together our position does not matter; for me the highest position is the one nearest to you. You must also surely have noticed in wills that unless someone has been a particular friend of one or the other of us we are left legacies of the same kind and value. All this shows that our love should be still warmer, seeing that there are so many ties to bind us in our work, character and reputation, and, above all, in the last wishes of our friends.

This is remarkable testimony to the character, not only of Tacitus, but of Pliny himself. The book referred to in the first sentence is either the *Dialogue* or one of the books of the *Histories*.

In VIII:7, Pliny replies to Tacitus, who had sent him a book of his to read, and Pliny agrees to give him his criticism. In the letter he speaks of Tacitus as the master and of himself as the pupil, *magister* and *discipulus*.

In IX:10, Pliny remarks that his summer holiday is a mixture of pleasure and literary activity. He has been writing poetry, and notes Tacitus's belief that poems are easily produced *inter nemora et lucos*, "in the woods and groves," which may be a reference to an expression of Tacitus in the *Dialogue* and therefore a clue to the date of the completion of that work and to its certain Tacitean authorship. Letter IX:14, another brief note to Tacitus, comments once again upon the close relationship between them.

You are never satisfied with yourself, but I never write with such confidence as when I write about you. Whether posterity will give us a thought I don't know, but surely we deserve one—I don't say for our genius, which sounds like boasting, but for our application, hard work, and regard for future generations. Only let us continue along the path we have chosen; if it leads few to the full light of fame, it brings many out of the shades of obscurity.

The first of the letters dealing with history and literature is I:20. Pliny argues at length for the preference among both the Greeks and the Romans for lengthy speeches. We know from Pliny's *Panegyricus* and his own performance in the prosecution of Marius Priscus that he was indeed a man who practiced what he preached. Yet at the end of the letter he says that he suspects that Tacitus will not agree with him and, if this is the case, he hopes that Tacitus will indicate his reasons. It does not, I think, take much imagination to surmise what Tacitus's judgment on this question was; he was a man who, in his historical work, was the master of brevity and epigram.

The next two letters, VI:16 and VI:20, are long and of the highest value. They were written in response to a request from Tacitus for information to be used in the *Histories* upon which he was then working, information about the eruption of Vesuvius in the year 79, the actions and the death of the elder Pliny, and the activities of the younger Pliny. In the first of the pair Pliny replies that he is delighted to give Tacitus the details at his disposal because he foresees that his uncle's death will be made immortal if it is incorporated in Tacitus's history: *nam video morti eius si celebretur a te immortalem gloriam esse propositam.* He continues a little bit later that Tacitus is writing for all time: *scriptorum tuorum aeternitas.* The next, about Pliny's own activities, adds nothing about Tacitus, but this is not surprising since this second letter is really no more than a continuation of the first.

The last letter in this group, VII:33, begins with a statement of praise for Tacitus, praise with which Pliny wishes to ally himself. He says, "I believe that your histories will be immortal: a prophecy which will surely prove correct" (*Auguror, nec me fallit augurium, historias tuas immortales futuras*). Consequently, he sends Tacitus a narrative about his own role in the trial of Baebius Massa in the year 93, which he hopes Tacitus will be able to incorporate in the *Histories*.

Biographical information is first presented in II:1, a letter addressed to his friend Voconius Romanus discussing the death and funeral of Verginius Rufus. Pliny remarks that the funeral was one that brought credit to the age and to the emperor and that the funeral oration was delivered by the consul, Cornelius Tacitus. This was Verginius's final stroke of good fortune; his life had been full of years and honors, and at his death his praises were pronounced by a most eloquent orator, a *laudator eloquentissimus*.

In II:11, Pliny writes in great detail of the notorious trial of Marius Priscus. He mentions that Tacitus and he were charged to serve as counsel for the provincials and then, toward the end of the letter (17), comments that the final rebuttal was delivered by Tacitus: *Respondit Cornelius Tacitus eloquentissime et, quod eximium orationi eius inest, σεμνῶς.* "Cornelius Tacitus made an eloquent speech in reply, with all the majesty which characterizes his style of oratory." Further, when the case was over, the consul-designate stated that Tacitus and Pliny had conscientiously and boldly performed the charge assigned them and had appropriately carried out their duties.

IV:15 is addressed to Minicius Fundanus. It is a letter of recommendation for a young man whose high qualities are particularly revealed because he is a friend of Tacitus; Pliny adds, parenthetically, "You know the sort of man Tacitus is," *scis quem virum*.

The last letter, IX:23, is a worthy culmination of this personal collection. It is addressed to a man named Maximus; Pliny comments upon occasions in his life when he has received pleasure from public recognition. When he has pleaded before the court of the *centumviri*, when he has delivered addresses in the Senate, he has been greeted with extraordinary applause and enthusiasm. But the one incident that gave him the greatest satisfaction of all had recently been told him by Tacitus. At the last series of races in the circus, Tacitus sat next to a Roman knight. After varied conversation, the man asked Tacitus whether he was an Italian or a provincial. Tacitus replied, "You know me from your reading." The knight continued. "Then are you Tacitus or Pliny?" *Tacitus es an Plinius?* And Pliny continues, "I can't tell you how delighted

I am to have our names assigned to literature as if they belonged there and not to individuals, and to learn that we are both known by our writing to people who would otherwise not have heard of us."

These are precious bits of information. We know nothing more about Tacitus's home life or his wife although, in the one place in the biography of her father where he mentions her, he does so in the most glowing terms. We do not know if he had any children. The impression that one often gets from reading his histories is that he was a gloomy, pessimistic, bitter man; yet the picture that Pliny gives us is that of a person quite the opposite.

There remains one additional piece of evidence. Pliny stated, as mentioned above, that he and Tacitus were frequently joined in wills. We have a substantial portion of such a will of a man named Dasumius; he evidently came from Cisalpine Gaul and, at his death in 108, left his estate to a very large number of heirs. Among those are two men, joined together, whose names, alas, are not fully recorded. The first one is *Secundo*, the second *Cornelio* (*CIL* VI, 10229, l. 17). It surely is not rash to assume that the former is Plinius Secundus and the latter Cornelius Tacitus.

The life and career that have been sketched show Tacitus appropriately against the background of his age. He was a man truly involved in the government of empire. Like his father-in-law Agricola, like the Emperor Trajan, he was either provincial or northern Italian in birth, not a member of the old aristocracy, who had come to Rome to pursue a public career and to offer the vigor and talent of the provincials from the west to the service of Rome. He was also a man who clearly moved with ease in the highest social level of the state. That he was chosen by Agricola as his son-in-law when barely twenty or even younger, that three emperors in succession marked him for public office at an age perhaps as early as he could reasonably have expected (considering that he was a provincial), and that he is listed among the grand roster of Dasumius's legatees all indicate that he was one of the new aristocracy. This is important not only to enable us to get a sense of the individual, but also to underscore the intimate knowledge that he obviously had of the workings of government and society. He was not a man who turned to history in mature years in despair, as Sallust had done because his public career was stymied. Rather, he felt a deeper sense that the career which he had up to that point pursued perhaps held no further reward and that it was more important for him, with the talent and insight that he possessed, to attempt to sketch the history of that empire, at least in part, which he had done his best to serve.

In antiquity, as far as one can tell, history tended to be written by men who had taken part in public life. Thucydides and Polybius had both commanded armies or held high office among their people. In Rome the elder Cato had a career perhaps second to none among his contemporaries. Pollio and Sallust are further antecedents; Livy is the exception, and his naiveté is often revealed precisely because he had never participated in the inner workings of government.

Tacitus was a senator with access to the senatorial files, with a personal acquaintance of many people, and opportunity to make inquiry concerning events as, for example, in his request to Pliny to give him details surrounding the eruption of Vesuvius. His public life and political career suited him surpassingly well to write a history as penetrating as any in antiquity since the great work of Thucydides.

III. THE
MINOR WORKS

Early in 98, Tacitus published his first work. It was a biography of his father-in-law, Gnaeus Julius Agricola. Agricola was a remarkable man, as great, it might be said, as a private citizen could be in this age. He was born in A.D. 40. His political career is marked by a steady advance through the *cursus honorum*, culminating in the consulship at an age some five years before the normal or customary year, although it is difficult to speak of a norm during the principate when a man could advance by as many as ten years depending upon the prestige of his family and the number of children whom he sired, since each child brought remission of one year from the minimum age.

Agricola's first public duties were in Britain as military tribune in 60, followed by the quaestorship in 64, when he served in Asia, a tribunate of the plebs in 66, and a praetorship in 68. That year saw the beginning of the upheaval of civil war, and before long he cast his lot with the party of Vespasian, a wise choice as later events proved. In 70 he was returned to Britain as commander of *legio XX Valeria Victrix*, and followed this tour of duty with the governorship of Aquitania as *legatus Augusti pro praetore*, with praetorian rank, from 74 to 76. He was recalled to Rome to undertake the highest post of the regular *cursus* as suffect consul in 77. In that year he married his daughter to Tacitus and received the high honor of a major priesthood, being appointed a pontifex. Then, either in the same year or the following one, he went for the third time to Britain, this time as *legatus Augusti pro praetore*, with consular rank, where for seven years as governor he accomplished some of Rome's most spectacular military achievements.

After his recall by Domitian, whether for reasons of military and political expediency or because of jealousy, he held no further public office, passing up the governorship of Asia, which he rightly could have considered his due, in the year 90. He died three years later at fifty-three, a figure of some import in his own day who, nonetheless, looms much larger for us than any other Roman during the long span of the principate with the exception of the emperors and members of the imperial families, for his son-in-law's hope that the reputation of his wife's father would survive the passage of time was fulfilled. Tacitus's tribute to Agricola was the gift of immortality.

The monograph is easily divided into sections, wherein biography and history are presented in alternate layers as well as being interwoven even in the most obviously biographical parts. It begins with a prooemium covering three chapters. Agricola's birth, early life and training, and his political career up to his governorship of Britain occupy chapters four through nine. The next three are concerned with the geography of the island and ethnography of its peoples, and chapters thirteen through seventeen survey the history of Rome's relations with Britain and the achievements of Agricola's predecessors. The main and central part of the work covers approximately half its entire length; it details the campaigns and administrative achievements of Agricola in chapters eighteen through thirty-eight, and is highlighted by the powerful speeches of Calgacus and Agricola in chapters thirty through thirty-four. Chapters thirty-nine through forty-three relate his recall and the last years of his life. An epilogue of three chapters, forty-four through forty-six, balances the prooemium.

What kind of work is this? There has been much controversy among scholars about the genre into which it should be set. It is, of course, a biography, but a biography unlike any other in antiquity. It has some characteristics of a *laudatio funebris*, the address delivered at the funeral of a distinguished person in which his career and merits are traced. We can imagine Tacitus's skill in this branch of literature from the impact his eulogy at the funeral of Verginius Rufus had upon the younger Pliny.

It has also been suggested that the *Agricola* is an example of a class of literature that became popular in the first century of the principate, detailing the death of famous men, the *exitus virorum illustrium*. This genre was extremely popular, for it furnished opportunity to express opposition to the principate by means of praise of those who had been its opponents. The *Agricola*, however, seems in spite of its peculiarity to fit most properly into the category of biography. It is much more than a funerary laudation, and it certainly has a far broader scope and intent than merely the record of an eminent man's death. Yet it is a new kind of biography, for biography, as best exemplified in Latin by Suetonius, tends to group personal characteristics to obtain a consistent or full presentation of the individual. There is no concern for chronology nor is there any intent to present a coherent life. Rather the subject is treated first from one point of view and then another, so that the reader may understand the individual, but he often does not understand or even receive information about the actions of that person in relation to the times and his own character.

The *Agricola* is ruthlessly chronological with a number of historical excurses, and the author allows himself to break into his narrative at the beginning, at the end, and in a very important passage at the conclusion of chapter forty-two. Biography the monograph is, to be sure, but there is also a very large part of history, and it is this which makes the work so uniquely important as the first essay of the man whom most critics will judge Rome's greatest historian. The theme of the work is much more than the presentation of the life of his father-in-law. It is political literature of the highest import in the early empire, a period during which, it has frequently been said, there was no political literature. Lucan's *Pharsalia* would of itself perhaps deny that claim, with the *Agricola* a strong ally.

An underlying theme of the work is the presentation of the way in which men can serve the state, the principate, without compromising their own *dignitas;* indeed, many were able to pursue distinguished careers. Whether one liked the empire or not was, in the last analysis, an irrelevant question. The empire was there and, although emperors changed, there was never any real opportunity after the first half of the first century A.D. that the form of government would disappear. That being the case, if a man disliked the principate, should he completely withdraw from involvement in the government of empire? Some said yes, and by their obstinate resistance to the ruler of the state gained for themselves recognition without, however, having accomplished anything of import. Yet a body of government as vast as the Roman Empire required administrators on all levels, and it is these men who are the largely unsung and anonymous heroes of the empire, who may have retained a spirit compatible with the freer and more exciting days of the late republic but who did not, in spite of that, deny their talent to the service of the state. Such, clearly, were the Emperor Trajan, Agricola, and Tacitus himself.

We have, then, in this work much more than merely the historical record of one individual and his achievements presented against the broad background of one corner of empire. We have a political manifesto of behavior which might almost be called, borrowing Cicero's title, *De officiis,* a treatise on political duties in the days of the principate.

The first three chapters, the prooemium, are the most crucial in the entire work for penetrating into the judgment of Tacitus himself. They deserve full presentation.

> The practice of recording for posterity the deeds and characters of famous men, which was common in times past, has not even in our own times been ignored by an age disdainful of its own people, whenever some great and outstanding excellence has overcome and risen above a fault common to states both great and small, that is, not to understand and yet to hate that which is right. But, just as it was easy and there was greater opportunity among our ancestors to do deeds worthy of record, so everyone who was most renowned for talent was motivated only by the reward of a good conscience to transmit the record of excellence without partiality or de-

sire of personal gain. Many even considered it confidence in their characters rather than arrogance to relate their own lives, nor was that an indication of lack of integrity or a source of reproach for Rutilius or Scaurus; so greatly are examples of excellence most highly cherished in the very periods in which they are most easily produced. But now I have had to ask for pardon as I undertake to relate the life of a deceased man, pardon which I would not have sought had I intended to bring charges against him, so cruel and hostile to excellence are the times.

We read that it was a capital crime when Thrasea Paetus and Helvidius Priscus were praised by Arulenus Rusticus and Herennius Senecio, respectively, and that violence was directed not only against the authors themselves but also against their books, with the assignment given to the commission of three men to burn in the comitium and the forum the achievements of the most celebrated talents. Surely they thought that the voice of the Roman people and the independence of the senate and the conscience of the human race were destroyed by that fire; and, in addition, they expelled the philosophers and drove all intellectual activity into exile, so that nothing honorable might anywhere meet one's gaze. We certainly displayed extraordinary submission, and just as a former age witnessed the extreme of liberty, so did we the extreme of slavery, when even the opportunity to speak and listen was wrested from us by espionage. We would also have lost our very memories, together with freedom of speech, if it were equally in our power to forget as to be silent.

Now at last our spirit returns; and although the Emperor Nerva, at the very beginning of a most happy age, united two things formerly incompatible, the rule of one man and personal freedom, and although the Emperor Trajan daily increases the good fortune of the times, and although the well–being of the people has not only expressed hope and a prayer for the future but has also received the fulfillment and realization of the prayer itself, yet by the nature of human weakness remedies are slower to take effect than their ills. And as our bodies grow slowly and are quickly destroyed, so too could one more readily crush genius and its activities than bring them back; for a certain pleasure in doing nothing comes over one, and the slothfulness that is hated at first is at the last esteemed. What if, for a period of fifteen years, a great span of human life, many men perished by natural deaths, and all the most capable because of the emperor's cruelty? We few indeed have outlived not only others but also, if I may use the expression, ourselves, with so many years plucked from the middle of our lives, years in which those of us who were young reached maturity, and the mature approached the very limits of extreme old age, in silence. Nonetheless, it will not be a source of regret to have written down the recollection of our former servitude and the record of our present good, even with a style unskilled and crude. This book, in the meantime, intended to honor my father-in-law, Agricola, will be praised for or excused by its expression of filial devotion.

The beginning of the third chapter is particularly significant. Tacitus comments that the Emperor Nerva has united two things which were formerly incompatible, the rule of one man and personal freedom: *Nerva Caesar res olim dissociabiles miscuerit, principatum ac libertatem.* How seriously are we to take this? It is my view that it must be taken very seriously indeed. Tacitus was writing in the glorious days of fresh air and newly won freedom after the murder of Domitian. His belief in the empire as a form of government had remained secure in spite of the battering it took at the hands of a bad emperor. Now, with the accession of a good one and the promise of an even better successor, his reception of the new age was sincere and heartfelt. There is to my mind no question but that at this point, even if he was less than totally enthusiastic about the empire, he at least accepted it and supported it with his best judgment.

A recurring tendency of much of Latin literature during both the republic and the empire is to present varying conceptions of empire, either in the author's own words or through a spokesman; on the whole many of these judgments are unfavorable. It may be that this is inevitable from a psychological point of view. Tacitus, who is perhaps one of the most outspoken imperialists and believers in the destiny of Rome that had been forecast in Vergil's great epic, particularly in the first book of the *Aeneid* when Jupiter promises Venus that Rome will have empire without limit, *imperium sine fine dedi* (279), has nonetheless presented perhaps the most outspoken indictment of Rome's empire that has yet been produced. He placed a long attack in the mouth of a Scottish chieftain named Calgacus, who harangues his followers before the decisive battle at Mons Graupius, the ultimate struggle before all Britain falls under the rule of Rome. His speech covers three chapters, thirty through thirty-two. The first of these is the most significant because it is the most emotional.

> As often as I consider the causes of war and our dire straits, I have great confidence that this day and your union will be the beginning of freedom for all Britain; for you have all joined together, you who have not experienced slavery, for whom there are no lands further on and not even the sea is safe, with the Roman fleet threatening us. Thus battle and weapons, which are honorable for the brave, are likewise the greatest source of safety even for cowards. Earlier struggles, in which we fought against the Romans with varying success, had a hope of assistance at our hands, since we, the noblest people of all Britain and for that reason living in its innermost sanctuary and not gazing upon any shores of those in slavery, kept our eyes also free from the contagion of conquest. Us, the most distant people of the earth and of liberty, our very isolation and the obscurity of our renown have protected up to this day: now the farthest boundary of Britain lies open, and everything unknown is considered marvelous, but now there are no people further on, nothing except waves and rocks, and the Romans more hostile than these, whose arrogance you would in vain try to avoid by obedience and submission. Plunderers of the world, after they, laying everything waste, ran out of land, they search out the sea: if the enemy is wealthy, they are greedy, if he is poor, they seek prestige, men whom neither the East nor the West has sated: they alone of all men desire wealth and poverty with equal enthusiasm. Robbery, butchery, rapine they call empire by euphemisms, and when they produce a wasteland, they call it peace.

The end is indeed the climax: *ubi solitudinem faciunt, pacem appellant.* Tremendously powerful and vigorous, it may hint at Tacitus's recognition of some possible faults of empire, but it is surely not his own view. He would hardly, himself a Roman, allow his judgment of Rome's empire to be presented by a barbarian. One must look elsewhere, throughout the entire corpus of his work, but particularly at one splendid speech in *Histories* IV:73–74, in which a Roman general and consul offers a reasoned defense of Rome's empire, clearly underscoring that everything good may be balanced by something bad.

Tacitus's dramatic sense leads him to follow the culminating triumph at Mons Graupius, and the events subsequent to it, with the fear that possessed Domitian, a fear that rose from the grand success of a man who might, indeed, have been considered a rival. He realized that Agricola was terribly popular and was in control of an army that was skilled in warfare and devoted to him. He recognized further that Agricola possessed a quality that was an imperial prerogative, that of being a great general. This appears in chapter thirty-nine where Tacitus writes, *cetera utcumque facilius dissimulari, ducis boni imperatoriam virtutem esse* (other talents were rather easily disregarded, one way or another, but to be a good general was the mark of an emperor). Domitian himself was not a general of the highest rank, whatever credit one may wish to give him for his Germanic campaigns. Agricola was consequently recalled (although strategic reasons may also have had their importance) and permitted to retire into private life without even having, after the passage of some half-dozen years, the governorship of Asia or Africa, the crowning glory of a senatorial career. Agricola was persuaded not to offer himself for either of these posts by the most obvious threats and the greatest disdain on the part of the emperor, as detailed in chapter forty-two.

This chapter concludes with what we might consider Tacitus's own political creed. "Let those whose custom it is to admire actions that are forbidden know that great men can exist even under bad emperors; and allegiance and moderation, if hard work and vigorous action are added, can reach the same level of renown that many have reached by dangerous paths, but they became famous by an ostentatious death, with no advantage to the state." *Sciant, quibus moris est illicita mirari, posse etiam sub malis principibus magnos viros esse, obsequiumque ac modestiam, si industria ac vigor adsint, eo laudis excedere, quo plerique per abrupta, sed in nullum rei publicae usum ambitiosa morte inclaruerunt.* Here, obviously, is Tacitus's view of those Stoics and other philosophers who prided themselves upon absolute resistance to any form of domination, but who thereby accomplished nothing for the common weal. As Tacitus said of Thrasea Paetus in a different context (*Ann.* XIV: 12,1), "imperilling himself, without communicating to the other senators any impulse towards freedom" (*sibi causam periculi fecit, ceteris libertatis initium non praebuit*).

Agricola clearly belongs to these "great men"; so do Tacitus and Pliny. All reached the high point of the consulate and served emperors both good and bad. So too did Trajan, who is linked with Agricola at the end of chapter forty-four, in the description of the latter's death, when Tacitus says, "For, although it was not permitted for him to live to see this light of a most happy age and to see Trajan as emperor, a circumstance that he used to forecast in our hearing with prophecy and prayers, yet he has as considerable compensation for his hastened death the fact that he escaped that last period, in which Domitian drained the state, no longer at intervals and with respites of time, but with, as it were, one continuous blow."

The last chapter, forty-six, must rank as one of the most noble and lofty pieces of Latin prose, perhaps rivalling Cicero's *Dream of Scipio* from the *De republica.* There is much commonplace material here, particularly concerning the belief in an afterlife, that was surely not unique to Tacitus. Yet it is, in a way, a Roman's recognition of what was really important in a Roman's life. It is not only what one does but also the kind of individual one was and the influence one had upon kin and friends that matter. The final sentence is a worthy culmination of the work. "Whatsoever in Agricola we loved and admired, that remains and is going to remain in the minds of men, in the never-ending span of time, by the glory of his achievements; for oblivion has overwhelmed many men of old as if they were without glory and of no rank: Agricola will survive, his story told and transmitted to posterity."

The publication of the *Agricola* was followed almost immediately by that of the *Germany,* an ethnographical treatise (for so it seems best to take it), which may indeed have had its genesis in the preceding year. Whether Tacitus had an ulterior motive in writing this work is a question that cannot be answered with any certainty. Many scholars think that it contains veiled advice or even a warning for the newly destined emperor Trajan, then resident on the Rhine frontier, by underscoring the Germans' threat to Rome and by suggesting that they were Rome's greatest potential danger.

Yet it seems unlikely that a mere senator, and one not greatly experienced in military matters, would undertake to offer advice to the masterful general. Nor does it appear probable that the monograph was a preliminary effort to gather material about Germany which was to be used in such graphic detail and vividness in the large works which were to follow. For whatever reason, Tacitus was evidently intrigued by this "noble" people to such a degree that he decided to pass on the results of his researches to the educated aristocracy of Rome.

There is no evidence that Tacitus ever saw Germany himself; we can thus with surety exclude first-hand experience as a source of his information. His chief debt was to Pliny the Elder's history of the wars in Germany in which the latter had taken part; this was supplemented by details obtained from merchants and travelers who had visited the North. The writing of the ethnography of a country or people had a lengthy tradition, and Tacitus tried his hand at it in this work.

The structure of the *Germany* is considerably simpler than that of the *Agricola*. The work falls naturally into two halves of almost equal length: the first considers, in general, the land and its people, their customs and practices in chapters one through twenty-seven; the second discusses the description of the individual tribes in chapters twenty-eight through forty-six. But each of these two main divisions can be broken down further. The general treatment devotes the first five chapters to geographical description of the land and to the origin of the people; the next ten chapters deal with public institutions, the following twelve with those of private life. The public and private sections are almost precisely the same in length.

Tacitus's consideration of the individual tribes is not a random presentation; chapters twenty-eight through thirty-seven deal with the tribes of the West and Northwest, generally following the line of the Rhine from south to north. The remainder of the work covers the Suebic tribes of the East and

North, generally following the course of the Danube from west to east before he jumps, as he must, to the almost fairy tale lands of the Far North. Again both parts are treated in almost the same length, although the amount of detail that Tacitus can present gradually diminishes as he moves farther away from the parts of Germany well known to the Romans through warfare and commerce.

There are two passages that perhaps seem out of place in an ethnographical essay; they verge rather upon history. The first appears at the end of chapter thirty-three, where Tacitus meditates upon the future of Rome's empire after he has reported the almost total annihilation of the Bructeri. This annihilation was accomplished by other Germanic peoples without any involvement of the Romans, who looked upon the event as if watching games in the amphitheater. The interpretation of this passage, to gain insight into Tacitus's thoughts on historiography and Rome's survival, will be discussed below.

The other is the long excursus (chapter thirty-seven) on Rome's two centuries and more of warfare and trial to conquer the Germans. Since the latter days of the second century B.C., Tacitus says, they have tested Rome's mettle and fought on equal terms with her armies; the freedom of the Germans is a greater danger than the royal dynasty of the Parthians, and no other enemy in time past had proved so unconquerable. Indeed, although Tacitus does no more than hint it, it may well be that the defeat inflicted by Arminius, the first great national German hero, upon Varus and his three legions in the Teutoburg Forest in A.D. 9 was the most potent setback in Rome's history up to that time. Previous disasters, such as the Caudine Forks against the Samnites in 321 B.C., Cannae against Hannibal and the Carthaginians in 216, and Arausio against the Cimbri and Teutons in 105, only delayed the outcome in each instance; Rome was, in a matter of years, ultimately victorious. But Varus's overwhelming loss changed Roman foreign policy fundamentally. The campaigns of Augustus's stepsons, Drusus and Tiberius, the later emperor, in the score of years on either side of the beginning of the Christian era, were intended to extend Rome's boundary against the unconquered tribes of Germany from the Rhine to the Elbe. After Varus's loss of his three legions whose numbers—XVII,

XVIII, and XIX—never again appeared in the legionary rosters, Augustus became content with the Rhine frontier; and future operations against the Germans, as those by Domitian, were generally concerned rather with consolidation of this Rhine line by shortening the salient between the Rhine and the Danube and establishing a defended border known as the *limes*. Only Marcus Aurelius was to have a larger vision once again. Suetonius tells the pathetic story of Augustus wandering around his residence, repeating again and again, "Varus, Varus, give me back my legions" (*The Deified Augustus*, XXIII:2). The effect upon all subsequent history of the reduction of Rome's German aspirations has been significant. Had the Germans been exposed to the same pacifying influences that moderated the martial nature of the Gauls, the world might have been spared the many tests of strength between German and Frenchman. In this chapter Tacitus rises far above the level of ethnography with the insight and judgments of the true historian.

Within the work there are only a few passages which are of more than particular interest. The first comes at the end of chapter two, where Tacitus explains how the Germans got their name. The text itself is much vexed, and of course any interpretation is therefore less than secure. It is worth quoting the Latin: *ceterum Germaniae vocabulum recens et nuper additum, quoniam qui primi Rhenum transgressi Gallos expulerint ac nunc Tungri, tunc Germani vocati sunt: ita nationis nomen, non gentis evaluisse paulatim, ut omnes primum a victore ob metum, mox etiam a se ipsis invento nomine Germani vocarentur.* "But the name of Germany is recent and lately introduced, since those who were the first to cross the Rhine and drive out the Gauls and are now called the Tungri were then called the Germani: so gradually the name of a tribe, not of a people, prevailed, with the result that all the people, at first called Germani by the victorious tribe in order to inject fear into the Gauls, soon gave themselves the same name after it had been invented." The conclusions about this passage have been a matter of the utmost concern to German scholars for several centuries. This work is beyond question the most popular classical work in Germany, and has been so for many years.

It has also been suggested that one of Tacitus's purposes in writing this work was to express his feelings about the magnificent morality of a people still uncorrupted by the vices of civilization. He thus looks back to a golden age and presents to the people of his own day in Rome a picture of the same kind of uncorrupted morality as did Livy when he wrote of the early history of the city.

There is a long passage, beginning at the end of chapter seventeen and running through the following two chapters, which perhaps most fairly presents Tacitus's views concerning the comparison of the more primitive, yet better, customs of the Germans and the present mores of the Romans.

And the women have the same garb as the men, except that the women are more often dressed in linen clothes and embroider them with purple, and do not fashion part of the upper garment into sleeves, but the whole arm is bare; and the adjacent part of the breast is also exposed.

In spite of this, marriages there are strict, and one would praise no other aspect of their civilization more. For almost alone of the barbarians they are content with one wife apiece with only a very few exceptions, who are the objects of many offers of marriages not because of their own lust but on account of their high rank. The wife does not bring a dowry to the husband, but rather the reverse occurs. Parents and relatives are present and pass judgment upon the gifts, gifts not suited to womanly pleasure nor with which the new bride may deck herself out, but cattle and a bridled horse and a shield with *framea* and sword. In return for these gifts a wife is obtained, and she in turn brings the man some weapon: they consider this exchange of gifts their greatest bond, these their sacred rites, these their marriage divinities. So that the woman may not think herself beyond the contemplation of brave acts and unaffected by the disasters of wars, she is reminded by the very first ceremonies with which her marriage begins that she comes as a partner in labors and dangers, who will suffer and dare the same thing as her husband in peace, the same thing in war: this the yoked oxen, this the caparisoned horse, this the gift of arms declare. So must she live and die, with the understanding that she is receiving things she is to hand on to her children, unimpaired and in worthy state, which her daughters-in-law may receive and which may be handed on again to grandchildren.

As a result, they live with chastity secured, corrupted by no attractions of games, by no seductions of banquets. Men and women are alike ignorant of secret correspondence. Although their population is so great, there are very few cases of adultery, the punishment for which is immediate and left to the husbands; in the presence of her relatives, the husband drives her naked from the home, with her hair cut off, and whips her through the whole village; indeed, there is no pardon for prostituted chastity; such a woman would not find a husband regardless of her beauty, youth, or wealth. There no one laughs at vices, and corruption and being corrupted are not excused by invoking the "times." Indeed, those states are still better in which only virgins marry and the hope and prayer of a wife are accomplished once and for all. Thus they receive one husband as they have received one body and one life, that there may be no further thought on the matter, no continuing desire, that they may esteem not their husbands, so to speak, but the state of marriage. It is considered a crime to limit the number of children or to put to death any of the children born after the first, and here good customs have greater influence than good laws elsewhere.

What Tacitus is particularly bitter about is that in Germany there is no corruption. Unlike the situation at Rome, where it is considered the fashionable thing, it is not a characteristic of the time: *nec corrumpere nec corrumpi saeculum vocatur*. The Germans may indeed have the advantage here, but not everything is better in Germany. Indeed, the Chatti, the most impressive of the German tribes, are described as the only ones who fight in a manner comparable to that of the Romans (chapter thirty). It is the Roman *disciplina* which has enabled Rome, in spite of all, to have the upper hand in her relations with Germany.

Beyond these are the Chatti, whose territory begins at the Hercynian Forest, where the country is not as flat and swampy as that of the other states that Germany embraces in its extent, since the hills extend through their territory and only gradually become less frequent, and the Hercynian Forest accompanies its Chatti to its limits and sets them down. The tribe is distinguished by hardier bodies, sinewy limbs, a threatening countenance and greater liveliness of mind. Considering that they are Germans, they have considerable judgment and skill: they choose their commanders and obey them, know how to keep their ranks, recognize opportunities, delay their attacks, map out the day, entrench themselves at night, consider fortune doubtful but bravery sure, and, a thing that is a very rare trait and one not granted except to Roman discipline, they place more confidence in the general than in the army. All their strength is in the infantry, whom they load down with tools and provisions in addition to their arms: you would see others go off to battle, the Chatti, however, go off to war. Sallies and a chance fight are rare occurrences. Indeed it is the particular assignment of a cavalry force to win victory quickly and to withdraw quickly: speed is akin to terror, deliberateness is closer to resolute courage.

The end of chapter thirty-three is, in many respects, the most crucial passage in the entire work. It reads as follows: *maneat, quaeso, duretque gentibus, si non amor nostri, at certe odium sui, quando urgentibus imperii fatis nihil iam praestare fortuna maius potest quam hostium discordiam.* "Let there continue and endure, I pray, among foreign peoples, if not affection for us, at least hatred for one another, since, as the destiny of empire drives us on, fortune can furnish us nothing greater than the discord of the enemy." There has been a tendency among scholars to discern Tacitus's great gloom and despair about the empire's future here. Roman historiography in general is indeed somber, since the early days of Rome were the best, the most virtuous, and the most glorious; inasmuch as Rome, beginning as a modest community with many rivals, expanded to become the greatest power in the history of the ancient world, everything afterward tended to be worse. Yet it need not be that Tacitus followed that tradition at this point. He was writing at a time when the general feeling of the Roman people was one of optimism and anticipation. Domitian had been murdered and condemned to *damnatio memoriae*; Trajan was now the designated successor to Nerva and would soon himself be on the throne. At such a time a historian would hardly foresee disaster. On the contrary, it is rather, I think, a summons to renewed expansion of the empire and to another glorious era, when a great general and a revered princeps will reinvigorate the character of the Roman people and re-establish their prowess in the field. Trajan's earlier military achievements made this a quite reasonable expectation, and I myself prefer to consider this passage one in which Tacitus is optimistic and looks forward to the fates of the empire pushing Rome on to ever greater dominion.

Chapter thirty-seven has already been mentioned and discussed. Yet it is worth quoting because here above all appears a sense of the great respect that Tacitus and all Romans had for the Germans and what he perhaps hoped Trajan would be able to accomplish against them.

> Nearest the ocean the Cimbri, a state now small but great in glory, occupy the same projection of Germany. And there remain widely scattered traces of their ancient renown, camps of great size on both sides of the Rhine, by the extent of which one may measure even now the power and numbers of the tribe and the credibility of so great a migration. Our city was in its six hundred and fortieth year when the arms of the Cimbri were first heard of, in the consulship of Caecilius Metellus and Papirius Carbo. If we should count from that year to the second consulship of the Emperor Trajan, the sum is about two hundred ten years: for so long a time has the conquest of Germany been in progress. In the course of so extended a period there have been many disasters on both sides. Not the Samnites, not the Carthaginians, not Spain or Gaul, not even the Parthians have more often given us warning: for the liberty of the Germans is a greater threat than the kingdom of Arsaces. For with what else could the East mock us except the death of Crassus, and it itself was crushed under Ventidius with the loss of Pacorus? But the Germans robbed the Roman people of five consular armies one after another, with Carbo and Cassius and Aurelius Scaurus and Servilius Caepio and Mallius Maximus routed or captured, and even stripped Augustus of Varus and his three legions; and not without loss did Gaius Marius defeat them in Italy, the Deified Julius in Gaul, Drusus and Nero and

Germanicus in their own territories; soon the great threats of Gaius Caesar were turned to mockery. Then there was peace, until, when opportunity had been offered by our internal strife and civil wars, they stormed the winter quarters of legions and even aimed at the Gallic provinces; and when they had again been beaten, thereafter, in recent times, they appeared in triumphal processions rather than being actually conquered.

The work then begins gradually to fade away. As Tacitus goes further and further to the north and east, information becomes less reliable and less common and finally his narrative ends in the realm of make-believe, although he does again emphasize his scorn for servitude.

The *Dialogue on Orators* is the third and most controversial of Tacitus's works. His name is absent from it in manuscript, and its style differs from that of the other works so greatly that Tacitean authorship has been totally denied or, if granted, a date of approximately 80 has been proposed for it, when Tacitus would have been about twenty-five years old. The *Dialogue* is based on Ciceronian antecedents and is Ciceronian in style and vocabulary; sentences are long and periodic rather than short, brusque, and lapidary. The difference has been explained away by suggesting that Tacitus wrote the work in his youth and then, in the years of silence under Domitian, developed the style that was peculiarly his own. Not that the champions of non-Tacitean authorship were content even with this. The work which we have, they argued, was by Titinius Capito, or was the *De causis corruptae eloquentiae* (*On the Causes of the Decline of Oratorical Eloquence*) of the great master of rhetoric, Quintilian himself. These views have in recent years generally lost favor; perhaps the greatest change in Tacitean studies of the last generation is the acceptance of the work as genuinely Tacitus's and the down-dating of it by some thirty years. Today it is safe to say, *pace* a few diehards, that Tacitus wrote this strange work in the first decade of the second century A.D. It is dedicated to Fabius Justus, consul in 102; the presentation of a literary piece to a friend upon the occasion of a significant event in his life was not an uncommon practice in ancient times. That year may not be the precise one of composition; the range 102–107 may be safer. But the exact date is less important than the general period. How can one explain the style and the occasion?

It has already been mentioned that Tacitus played a key role in the prosecution of Marius Priscus in 100. His speech, Pliny said, had been marked with majesty (he had spoken σεμνῶς); and earlier, in the year 97, upon the occasion of Verginius Rufus's death, Tacitus gave the funeral address most eloquently (Pliny calls him *laudator eloquentissimus*). In September 100 Pliny delivered his long expression of thanks to the Emperor Trajan. Tacitus may well have determined during that year to withdraw from oratory to devote himself to a higher study, history, convinced that the great days of oratory were gone and that its chief purpose now was for display. Similarly, in the *Dialogue*, Maternus decided to retire from the law courts to spend his time on a higher pursuit, poetry. The relationship between poetry and history in antiquity was very close; Quintilian speaks of history as a kind of poetry without the exigencies of metrical form (x:1,31). Maternus, no doubt, represents the author in the discussion; the reasons given in his closing speech for the decline of oratory go well with Tacitus's views expressed throughout the other works. Pliny, puffed up with his great triumph of language and endurance, must have felt a little deflated when his friend and hero decided that oratory was a field no longer worthy of his talents. The *Dialogue*, then, might very well be Tacitus's swan song to oratory.

But why is the style so different from all else by Tacitus? The ability and capacity to write in various styles, almost, so to speak, to change clothes, were the marks of the trained rhetorician who realized that different genres of literature required different garbs. In a genre in which Cicero was the acknowledged master, nothing was more appropriate than the Ciceronian garb. Men can write different works in different styles at the same time; certainly one should no longer attempt to base a date for the *Dialogue* on its stylistic uniqueness in the corpus of Tacitus's works.

The theme of the *Dialogue on Orators* is clearly presented in the very first sentence. The question is raised regarding why oratory is now so much inferior to what it used to be. Tacitus uses the Ciceronian form of the dialogue to report artistically a discussion on this subject which he had heard when he was a young man. The participants are four of the most renowned speakers of the day. All of these except Messalla are provincial in origin, exemplifying the great influence that men from the provinces possessed. This is an evolution that culminated in the accession of the first non-Italian emperor, Trajan, barely twenty years after the dramatic date of this dialogue.

The scene is set at Curiatius Maternus's home; Marcus Aper and Julius Secundus call upon him the day after he has offended the feelings of very powerful men by the recitation of a play with views too liberal for the times. The first four chapters serve as introduction; Maternus states that he will give up his career as a pleader and devote himself exclusively to poetry. Aper, an enthusiastic and violent advocate of the new and modern style of oratory, argues fiercely in chapters five through ten that oratory is a more noble and useful occupation than poetry. Maternus rebuts him gently in chapters eleven through thirteen.

At this point, Vipstanus Messalla, the bearer of a great name of republican renown, enters and is apprised of the subject of discussion by Secundus. After stating that he had already devoted much thought to the subject, Messalla is asked to present his views. Messalla worships the achievements of the ancient orators; these feelings are assaulted by Aper in a long tirade covering chapters fifteen through twenty-three. Aper first sophistically argues that the word *ancient* should not be applied to Cicero and his contemporaries who lived but yesterday, as it were, and then severely criticizes all the orators of the republic for various serious failings. Messalla, in chapters twenty-five to twenty-seven (twenty-four serves as a bridge), defends them *in toto* against the claims of the "moderns." But he is then reminded by Maternus that he has not yet explained why oratory now falls below the level it achieved a century and more ago.

The main part of the work now begins. Messalla argues that the responsibility rests with the current modes of training and education of children. Contrary to the strict and practical training prevalent in days gone by, children are now raised by nurses and slaves and are then sent to schools of the rhetoricians, where they learn to speak prettily but to no purpose. They gain no experience in life.

Messalla is still speaking in chapter thirty-five when the text is broken by a lacuna. When the text begins anew, the speaker appears to be Maternus, who continues to hold forth until the end of the dialogue when the visitors depart in good humor. Maternus pinpoints the cause of oratory's decline in the changed political climate of the principate. In the chaos and anarchy of the last days of the republic, great policies of government were championed and thwarted by oratorical skill. But now, in the quiet days of the empire, all major decisions are made by the emperor, who is recognized as the single wisest person, *sapientissimus et unus.* With the absence of great issues oratory has flagged, but one should not mourn its decline, for the state is now lawfully ordered. One may detect a sigh for the changed order in Maternus's remarks, but there is no question of his acceptance of the good that the imperial form of government has produced.

More scholarly discussion has centered on the question of the lacuna than any other aspect of the work. Several points must be considered. In the view presented in the preceding paragraph, Secundus is left without any major role in the entire dialogue; indeed, he does nothing more than bring Messalla up-to-date when the latter appears. To many, this seems incomprehensible; they therefore assign him chapters thirty-six to forty (as far as the words *Non de otiosa*), postulate another lacuna before these words, and claim that this second gap contains the end of Secundus's speech and the beginning of Maternus's. The objection that there is no evidence in the manuscripts for a second lacuna seems to me to be fatal to this reconstruction; lacunae do not customarily begin neatly at the end of a sentence and conclude at the beginning of another. Since it it impossible to estimate how many pages of the manuscripts have been lost, scholars have argued for a long lacuna and hence a speech for Secundus, with or without another gap in chapter forty, and for a short lacuna and hence no possibility for a speech for Secundus. I agree with the latter, and the results of this view are presented above.

The work displays much good literary criticism. It is perhaps surprisingly harsh on Cicero, whose excesses and repetitions are brutally underscored, particularly in chapter twenty-two. Yet despite this, the conclusion which is boldly stated, and with which Aper would no doubt agree, is that there is no question but that the people of old were better speakers. Aper himself had mentioned that things were not always better in the past and worse in the present, but he does not seem to have sincerely believed that concerning oratory.

The question that still remains is why the supremacy of the orators of the past was unchallenged. There was, of course, in the olden days, a violence and freedom in political life which is now absent, and it is in this context that the answer is to be sought. The present may indeed be better than the past. At the end of the work, Maternus delivers what is almost a peroration, and it may not be inappropriate to see Tacitus himself in the figure of the great orator who retires from the battlefield of the court and forum. Maternus speaks of the calm and quiet of the present day, the principate, as *composita et quieta et beata res publica* (36,2) because of the presence of *moderator unus* (36,2), as *optimus civitatis status* (37,5), as a period of *longa temporum quies et continuum populi otium et assidua senatus tranquillitas et maxima principis disciplina* (38,2), as a time when decisions of state are made, not by the ignorant and inexperienced many, but by *sapientissimus et unus* (41,4). Granted that personal freedom has been impaired, granted that the seeds of great and fiery oratory have disappeared, in comparison with the turbulent days of the late republic (*non mos, non ius*) there was now a well-ordered commonwealth, and one cannot have everything: *nunc, quoniam nemo eodem tempore adsequi potest magnam famam et magnam quietem, bono saeculi sui quisque citra obtrectationem alterius utatur* (41,5). "Now, since no one can attain great renown and great repose at the same time, let each one enjoy the blessing of his own age without detracting from the other."

How is this great and peaceful state to be brought about? How is it to be maintained? The key is, of course, the emperor, and it is in the major works that Tacitus underscored the development of the principate and perhaps suggested the kind of man who should have ruled.

IV. THE MAJOR WORKS

When Tacitus published the *Dialogue*, he was already at work on the *Histories*, the subject of which was the events of the years 69 to 96. He must have spent much of this decade on the *Histories*, and then, perhaps after an interlude of some years, he turned to the *Annals*, in which he reverted to the death of Augustus and treated the history of the principate of Tiberius, Gaius (better known as Caligula), Claudius, and Nero, the years 14 to 68. These two works comprised thirty books, a figure recorded by St. Jerome. How they were divided is a matter of controversy. Tradition assigns fourteen to the *Histories*, sixteen to the *Annals*. But there are those who argue for a hexadic grouping of books. The *Histories* will then have contained twelve, six on Vespasian and six on Titus and Domitian, and the *Annals* eighteen, six on Tiberius, six on Gaius and Claudius, and six on Nero.

The *Histories*, in the fragmentary form in which they have survived to us, are a spacious work. A bit more than four books, I through part of V, covers less than two years, a coverage unmatched by any other ancient historian. The subject is of the utmost importance. It is in the last analysis little more than the Roman Empire's struggle for survival after the shock of the elimination of the Julio-Claudian dynasty, a struggle not only internal, with one claimant for the purple constantly challenging another, but also external against enemies whose attack upon the homogeneous fabric of the empire was greater than that at any time in the past. The year 69, as Tacitus put it, was almost the last year of the Roman state.

Tacitus begins with announcement of the year's consuls. His starting point is intriguing. Why does he commence with January 1, 69, rather than begin his narrative with the middle of the preceding year with either the uprising against Nero or the latter's suicide? The two major works combine to form continuous history from the death of Augustus in the latter part of 14 to the death of Domitian in 96, with the exception of some six months in 68. Why Tacitus would have chosen to begin his chief historical undertakings in this way is a question which has been much debated, particularly in recent years. Sallust had begun his *Histories* with January 1 of a crucial year, and Tacitus may consciously have followed this precedent. Yet, it may well be that he found the subject matter of the year 68 somewhat unattractive because, from the point of view of the Roman people, the prime figure in the challenge to Nero's rule was the eminent Verginius Rufus, whose funeral laudation, as we have already seen, Tacitus delivered in his consulate. Perhaps Tacitus found Verginius's role in these events not entirely creditable and therefore chose to remain silent about them rather than to record his disapproval. His relationship with the great man was not as close as Pliny's; his feelings about Verginius were clearly less enthusiastic than Pliny's.

Be that as it may, the announcement of the consuls of the year makes it obvious that we have a work of annals, where events will be described chronologically, year by year, in the grand tradition of Roman historiography. The work is introduced by a prooemium of eleven chapters; the first three chapters develop the philosophy of history that was first presented in the *Agricola*.

In these three chapters, Tacitus comments upon the difficulty of his task and the ghastly nature of his theme. It is a tale which does not make for happy reading; to write of it brings despair.

I begin my work with the time when Servius Galba was consul for the second time with Titus Vinius for his colleague. Of the former period, the 820 years dating from the founding of the city, many authors have treated; and while they had to record the transactions of the Roman people, they wrote with equal eloquence and freedom. After the conflict at Actium, and when it became essential to peace, that all power should be centered in one man, these great intellects passed away. Then too the truthfulness of history was impaired in many ways; at first, through men's ignorance of public affairs, which were now wholly strange to them, then, through their passion for flattery, or, on the other hand, their hatred of their masters. And so between the enmity of the one and the servility of the other, neither had any regard for posterity. . . .

I am entering on the history of a period rich in disasters, frightful in its wars, torn by civil strife, and even in peace full of horrors. Four emperors perished by the sword. There were three civil wars; there were more with foreign enemies; there were often wars that had both characters at once. There was success in the East, and disaster in the West. There were disturbances in Illyricum; Gaul wavered in its allegiance; Britain was thoroughly subdued and immediately abandoned; the tribes of the Suevi and the Sarmatae rose in concert against us; the Dacians had the glory of inflicting as well as suffering defeat; the armies of Parthia were all but set in motion by the cheat of a counterfeit Nero. Now too Italy was prostrated by disasters either entirely novel, or that recurred only after a long succession of ages; cities in Campania's richest plains were swallowed up and overwhelmed; Rome was wasted by conflagrations, its oldest temples consumed, and the Capitol itself fired by the hands of citizens. Sacred rites were profaned; there was profligacy in the highest ranks; the sea was crowded with exiles, and its rocks polluted with bloody deeds. In the capital there were yet worse horrors. Nobility, wealth, the refusal or the acceptance of office, were grounds for accusation, and virtue ensured destruction. The rewards of the informers were no less odious than their crimes; for while some seized on consulships and priestly offices, as their share of the spoil, others on procuratorships, and posts of more confidential authority, they robbed and ruined in every direction amid universal hatred and terror.

Slaves were bribed to turn against their masters, and freedmen to betray their patrons; and those who had not an enemy were destroyed by friends.

Yet the age was not so barren in noble qualities, as not also to exhibit examples of virtue. Mothers accompanied the flight of their sons; wives followed their husbands into exile; there were brave kinsmen and faithful sons in law; there were slaves whose fidelity defied even torture; there were illustrious men driven to the last necessity, and enduring it with fortitude; there were closing scenes that equalled the famous deaths of antiquity. Besides the manifold vicissitudes of human affairs, there were prodigies in heaven and earth, the warning voices of the thunder, and other intimations of the future, auspicious or gloomy, doubtful or not to be mistaken. Never surely did more terrible calamities of the Roman People, or evidence more conclusive, prove that the Gods take no thought for our happiness, but only for our punishment.

These chapters give us further insight into Tacitus's view of history. He makes it perfectly clear that even though his public career advanced under all three of the Flavian emperors, he is, nonetheless, able to speak without partiality and without prejudice: *sed incorruptam fidem professis neque amore quisquam et sine odio dicendus est.* Not all readers of the historian will agree that he attained this high level of integrity; this subject is discussed further in chapter nine. Tacitus also says that he proposes, if he should live long enough, to write the history of the principates of Nerva and of Trajan, a subject richer and less hazardous, because it is now possible for a man to think what he wants and to say what he thinks.

Chapters four through eleven anticipate the narrative proper. Tacitus presents a summary of the state of the empire to show what power and what resources there were when the great challenge first came. There is only one other place in his writings where he goes into comparable detail, offering the kind of material that modern historians, so concerned with social and economic factors, long to have. The place is at the beginning of the fourth book of the *Annals*.

In the present context he also offers one of his best-known

judgments, an expression of the kind that can easily be plucked from the narrative and used thereafter as a truism. The most significant emotional impact that stemmed from the uprising of the year 68 was the realization among all that an emperor could be made elsewhere than in Rome: *evolgato imperii arcano, posse principem alibi quam Romae fieri* (1:4,2).

These eight chapters have another purpose: to introduce briefly but adequately some of the main figures who people the narrative that is to come, namely Galba, Verginius, Vitellius, Mucianus, and Vespasian. When Tacitus has accomplished this, he closes the introduction as he had begun it, with mention of the consuls, but goes far beyond merely temporal indication with the terrible judgment that the year was almost the death knell of the Roman state: *hic fuit rerum Romanarum status, cum Servius Galba iterum Titus Vinius consules inchoavere annum sibi ultimum, rei publicae prope supremum.*

With chapter twelve begins the narrative of the month of January which was to mark, before many days had passed, the end of Galba's principate and life. His reign is marked by evil omens, by a mood of gloom and despair, by a monumental case of misguided judgment in the selection of a successor, and by the anachronism of his personality in an age which was no longer able to tolerate men such as he. His sense of discipline, honesty, and integrity was too great for a soldiery which had been corrupted by Nero. Galba was intrinsically a good man who meant well, but he was too unbending and he was not able to feel the public pulse. All this lost him favor; indeed, his entry into Rome (although earlier than the beginning of the narrative) had been inauspicious because of a massacre which ensued. Consequently it did not take much urging for those upon whom he had to rely most, the praetorian guard, to look elsewhere for a favorite.

The thirty-eight chapters which cover the reign of Galba in the first book of the *Histories* are a tragedy in every sense of the word. The obituary (1:49) with which Tacitus favors Galba is one of his finest pieces of writing. It delineates his great qualities as well as his shortcomings, and concludes with the damning judgment that, while he was a private citizen, he seemed greater than one, and, by the agreement of all, he was a man capable of ruling, if only he had not ruled: *maior privato visus, dum privatus fuit, et omnium consensu capax imperii, nisi imperasset.*

The downfall of Galba was accomplished by Otho, about whom no good man could realistically have been optimistic. He was a man whose private life and public career, in part at least, had forewarned against too great expectations. Nonetheless, in spite of faults, he was able to play the emperor astonishingly well. His address on the significance and grandeur of the Roman Senate (1:84) was perhaps never spoken by him and may fairly represent Tacitus's own views. Be that as it may, it is an admirable speech, particularly his comment that the Senate represents the immortality of the Roman state. But Otho, greedy for the purple, is in his turn overthrown and succeeded by a worse man. Yet his end was worthy of the great heroes of Rome's halcyon days. After his army has been defeated in the first battle of Bedriacum, he refuses to continue the struggle to prevent further Roman bloodshed on both sides. He speaks wisely and calmly to his associates and relatives, and then in the grand tradition commits suicide. Tacitus grants him a generous obituary, appropriate to his life and death (II:50): "By two daring acts, one most atrocious, the other singularly noble, he earned in the eyes of posterity about an equal share of infamy and of glory." The former refers to the murder of Galba, the latter to his suicide. From Tacitus, this is no mean praise.

The army that defeated Otho was championing the cause of Vitellius, son of the Emperor Claudius's great colleague, who had held three consulates, a mark of the utmost distinction in the empire, and had been censor with the emperor. The son, however, brought nothing to the throne save his father's repute. Vitellius was a debauché, perhaps the most incapable of all who had before him occupied the throne of the Caesars as rulers of this vast empire. His accession sets the stage for disaster; the expedition of his troops from Germany, led in two armies by Caecina and Valens, compounds the mood of fear and despair because they enter Italy like enemies coming to plunder rather than as armies of the Roman people. But soon we are introduced quite vividly to Vespasian. In

II:73, Tacitus reports that Vitellius vaunted himself in an astonishing manner after he had heard that the armies of Syria and Judaea had sworn allegiance to him. Vespasian's name was often in men's mouths, and Vitellius realized that he was a potential rival. "It would almost pass belief, were I to tell to what a degree the insolence and sloth of Vitellius grew upon him when messengers from Syria and Judaea brought the news that the provinces of the East had sworn allegiance to him. Though as yet all information was but vague and uncertain, Vespasian was the subject of much talk and rumour, and at the mention of his name Vitellius often roused himself. But now, both the Emperor and the army, as if they had no rival to fear, indulging in cruelty, lust, and rapine, plunged into all the license of foreign manners."

Tacitus then devotes six chapters to a detailed examination of the mind and mood of the eastern armies, commanded by Vespasian and Mucianus, and the latter's exhortation for Vespasian to claim the purple (II:76–77).

> Though staggered by these apprehensions, he was confirmed in his purpose by others among the legates and among his own friends, and particularly by Mucianus, who, after many conversations with him in private, now publicly addressed him in the following terms: "All who enter upon schemes involving great interests, should consider whether what they are attempting be for the advantage of the State, for their own credit, easy of accomplishment, or at any rate free from serious difficulty. They must also weigh the circumstances of their adviser, must see whether he will follow up his advice by imperilling himself, and must know who, should fortune prosper the undertaking, is to have the highest honours. I invite you, Vespasian, to a dignity which will be as beneficial to the State, as it will be honourable to yourself. Under heaven this dignity lies within your reach. And do not dread what may present the semblance of flattery. To be chosen successor to Vitellius would be more of an insult than a compliment. It is not against the vigorous intellect of the Divine Augustus, it is not against the profound subtlety of the aged Tiberius, it is not even against the house of Caius, Claudius, or Nero, established by a long possession of the Empire, that we are rising in revolt. You have already yielded to the prestige even of Galba's family. To persist in

inaction, and to leave the State to degradation and ruin, would look like indolence and cowardice, even supposing that servitude were as safe for you as it would be infamous. The time has gone by and passed away when you might have endured the suspicion of having coveted Imperial power. That power is now your only refuge. Have you forgotten how Corbulo was murdered? His origin, I grant, was more illustrious than ours; yet in nobility of birth Nero surpassed Vitellius. The man who is afraid sees distinction enough in any one whom he fears. That an Emperor can be created by the army, Vitellius is himself a proof, who, though he had seen no service and had no military reputation, was raised to the throne by the unpopularity of Galba. Otho, who was overcome, not indeed by skilful generalship, or by a powerful army, but by his own premature despair, this man has made into a great and deservedly regretted Emperor, and all the while he is disbanding his legions, disarming his auxiliaries, and sowing every day fresh seeds of civil war. All the energy and high spirit which once belonged to his army is wasted in the revelry of taverns and in aping the debaucheries of their chief. You have from Judaea, Syria, and Egypt, nine fresh legions, unexhausted by battle, uncorrupted by dissension; you have a soldiery hardened by habits of warfare and victorious over foreign foes; you have strong fleets, auxiliaries both horse and foot, kings most faithful to your cause, and an experience in which you excel all other men.

"For myself I will claim nothing more than not to be reckoned inferior to Valens and Caecina. But do not spurn Mucianus as an associate, because you do not find in him a rival. I count myself better than Vitellius; I count you better than myself. Your house is ennobled by the glories of a triumph; it has two youthful scions, one of whom is already equal to the cares of Empire, and in the earliest years of his military career won renown with these very armies of Germany. It would be ridiculous in me not to waive my claims to Empire in favour of the man whose son I should adopt, were I myself Emperor. Between us, however, there will not be an equal distribution of the fruits of success or failure. If we are victorious, I shall have whatever honour you think fit to bestow on me; the danger and the peril we shall share alike; nay, I would rather have you, as is the better policy, direct your armies, and leave to me the conduct of the war and the hazards of battle. At this very moment a stricter discipline prevails among the conquered than among the conquerors. The conquered are fired to valour by anger, by hatred, by the desire of vengeance, while the conquerors are losing their energy in pride and insolence. War will of itself discover and lay open the hidden and rankling wounds of the victorious party. And, indeed, your vigilance, economy, and wisdom, do not inspire me with greater confidence of success than do the indolence, ignorance, and cruelty of Vitellius. Once at war, we have a better cause than we can have in peace, for those who deliberate on revolt have revolted already."

Vespasian becomes convinced of his destiny by varied omens and gradually prepares his forces, with the assistance of Mucianus, for the march to the continent of Europe. Vespasian himself is in no haste. He is much more concerned with control of the granary that was Egypt with the intent, if the need should arise, of starving Italy into acceptance of his cause. Mucianus readies himself for the Italian campaign, but is anticipated by Antonius Primus, commander of the seventh legion along the Danube who, on his own initiative, begins a forced march into Italy.

Book III begins with this remarkable person, and for much of this momentous book he occupies center stage. His earlier career had been criminal, and his recovery of senatorial status ranked as one of the misfortunes of civil war. Yet he was an enthusiastic supporter of Vespasian's cause (*acerrimus belli concitator*) and his speedy and decisive initiative won the day. There are two main episodes in this book. One is the second battle of Cremona, which culminated in the defeat of Vitellius's forces and the total destruction and sack of the city. The other is the burning of the Capitol at Rome in the struggle between Vitellius and Flavius Sabinus, the brother of Vespasian, who was prefect of the city; Tacitus's description of this disaster is one of his masterpieces (III:71–72).

Martialis had hardly returned to the Capitol, when the infuriated soldiery arrived, without any leader, every man acting on his own impulse. They hurried at quick march past the Forum and the temples which hang over it, and advanced their line up the opposite hill as far as the outer gates of the

Capitol. There were formerly certain colonnades on the right side of the slope as one went up; the defenders, issuing forth on the roof of these buildings, showered tiles and stones on the Vitellianists. The assailants were not armed with anything but swords, and it seemed too tedious to send for machines and missiles. They threw lighted brands on a projecting colonnade, and following the track of the fire would have burst through the half-burnt gates of the Capitol, had not Sabinus, tearing down on all sides the statues, the glories of former generations, formed them into a barricade across the opening. They then assailed the opposite approaches to the Capitol, near the grove of the Asylum, and where the Tarpeian rock is mounted by a hundred steps. Both these attacks were unexpected; the closer and fiercer of the two threatened the Asylum. The assailants could not be checked as they mounted the continuous line of buildings, which, as was natural in a time of profound peace, had grown up to such a height as to be on a level with the soil of the Capitol. A doubt arises at this point, whether it was the assailants who threw lighted brands on to the roofs, or whether, as the more general account has it, the besieged thus sought to repel the assailants, who were now making vigorous progress. From them the fire passed to the colonnades adjoining the temples; the eagles supporting the pediment, which were of old timber, caught the flames. And so the Capitol, with its gates shut, neither defended by friends, nor spoiled by a foe, was burnt to the ground.

This was the most deplorable and disgraceful event that had happened to the Commonwealth of Rome since the foundation of the city; for now, assailed by no foreign enemy, with Heaven ready to be propitious, had our vices only allowed, the seat of Jupiter Supremely Good and Great, founded by our ancestors with solemn auspices to be the pledge of Empire, the seat, which neither Porsenna, when the city was surrendered, nor the Gauls, when it was captured, had been able to violate, was destroyed by the madness of our Emperors. Once before indeed during civil war the Capitol had been consumed by fire, but then only through the crime of individuals; now it was openly besieged, and openly set on fire. And what were the motives of this conflict? what the compensation for so great a disaster: was it for our country we were fighting? King Tarquinius Priscus had vowed its erection in his war with the Sabines, and had laid the foundations on a scale which suited the hopes of future greatness rather than what the yet moderate resources of Rome could achieve. After him, Servius Tullius, heartily assisted by the allies, and Tarquinius Superbus, employing the spoils of war from the conquered Suessa Pometia, raised the superstructure. But the glory of its completion was reserved for the days of liberty. After the expulsion of the Kings, Horatius Pulvillus, in his second consulate, dedicated it, a building so magnificent, that the vast wealth afterwards acquired by the people of Rome served to embellish rather than increase it. It was rebuilt on the same site, when, after an interval of 415 years, it was burnt to the ground in the consulate of Lucius Scipio and Caius Norbanus. Sulla, after his final triumph, undertook the charge of restoring it, but did not live to dedicate it, the one thing denied to his uniform good fortune. The name of Lutatius Catulus, the dedicator, remained among all the vast erections of the Emperors, down to the days of Vitellius. This was the building that was now on fire.

The psychological impact of the destruction of Jupiter's temple was great and widespread, for many, Romans and foreigners alike, believed that it presaged the end of the Roman State and Empire.

The first three books, constituting half the hexad, have been concerned with the civil war, the war of Roman against Roman, recalling the terrible days of the end of the Roman Republic, the period known as the Roman Revolution, when dynast challenged dynast until, with the battle of Actium, only one remained. Octavian, soon entitled Augustus, then established the principate which had survived without military challenge for almost precisely one hundred years. Now the claim of one aspirant after another was sucking the vital blood of the Roman Empire. At this point in his narrative, with the success of Vespasian, the last of the year 69's four emperors, Tacitus turns his attention to the uprising whence the original challenge to Nero had arisen: the revolt of Civilis in Gaul, which may well have begun only as an expression of dissatisfaction with Nero but which rapidly changed its character to challenge the very existence of the Empire. The military events are uniformly unfavorable to Rome throughout much of Book IV. Disaster follows upon disaster, with the result that many believed that the days of the empire's existence were numbered. And it is at this point, just as centuries earlier Polybius had chosen the dark days of the aftermath of Cannae to show why Rome had survived and to discourse on the strength of her constitution, that Tacitus puts a speech into the mouth of a Roman consular and general, Petilius Cerialis, which is one of the finest expressions extant of the rationale of the Roman Empire. It is this speech which must most particularly be balanced against the indictment of Calgacus in the *Agricola* (IV:73–74).

Cerialis then convoked an assembly of the Treveri and Lingones, and thus addressed them: "I have never cultivated eloquence; it is by my sword that I have asserted the excellence of the Roman people. Since, however, words have very great weight with you, since you estimate good and evil, not according to their real value, but according to the representations of seditious men, I have resolved to say a few words, which, as the war is at an end, it may be useful for you to have heard rather than for me to have spoken. Roman generals and Emperors entered your territory, as they did the rest of Gaul, with no ambitious purposes, but at the solicitation of your ancestors, who were wearied to the last extremity by intestine strife, while the Germans, whom they had summoned to their help, had imposed their yoke alike on friend and foe. How many battles we have fought against the Cimbri and Teutones, at the cost of what hardships to our armies, and with what result we have waged our German wars, is perfectly well known. It was not to defend Italy that we occupied the borders of the Rhine, but to insure that no second Ariovistus should seize the empire of Gaul. Do you fancy yourselves to be dearer in the eyes of Civilis and the Batavi and the Transrhenane tribes, than your fathers and grandfathers were to their ancestors? There have ever been the same causes at work to make the Germans cross over into Gaul, lust, avarice, and the longing for a new home, prompting them to leave their own marshes and deserts, and to possess themselves of this most fertile soil and of you its inhabitants. Liberty, indeed, and the like specious names are their pretexts; but never did any man seek to enslave his fellows and secure dominion for himself, without using the very same words.

"Gaul always had its petty kingdoms and intestine wars, till you submitted to our authority. We, though so often provoked, have used the right of conquest to burden you only with the cost of maintaining peace. For the tranquillity of nations cannot be preserved without armies; armies cannot exist without pay; pay cannot be furnished without tribute; all else is common between us. You often command our legions. You rule these and other provinces. There is no privilege, no exclusion. From worthy Emperors you derive equal advantage, though you dwell so far away, while cruel rulers are most formidable to their neighbours. Endure the passions and rapacity of your masters, just as you bear barren seasons and excessive rains and other natural evils. There will be vices as long as there are men. But they are not perpetual, and they are compensated by the occurrence of better things. Perhaps, however, you expect a milder rule under Tutor and Classicus, and fancy that armies to repel the Germans and the Britons will be furnished by less tribute than you now pay. Should the Romans be driven out (which God forbid) what can result but wars between all these nations? By the prosperity and order of eight hundred years has this fabric of empire been consolidated, nor can it be overthrown without destroying those who overthrow it. Yours will be the worst peril, for you have gold and wealth, and these are the chief incentives to war. Give therefore your love and respect to the cause of peace, and to that capital in which we, conquerors and conquered, claim an equal right. Let the lessons of fortune in both its forms teach you not to prefer rebellion and ruin to submission and safety."

Book v begins with an excursus on the Jewish State, as Tacitus returns once more to the war in Judaea, records the information that he had about the Jewish people and their religion, and makes quite clear his typically Roman dislike of everything connected with them; it continues with the Gallic campaign, which is now going in Rome's favor, and then breaks off. One can conjecture what the contents of the remainder of the *Histories* would have been. The subject would by no means have been as exciting as that treated in the four and one-half books that survive. The war in Gaul was rapidly brought to an end, as was that in Judaea, and Vespasian then undertook to consolidate the dynasty of his own family and to restore the Roman state to health.

The grand theme that Tacitus treats in the *Histories* is unmatched anywhere else in his work. One can almost assume that in a narrative detailing foreign wars Rome will ultimately triumph and will indeed be able to overcome any disagreements within herself. But in the years 68 and 69, Rome's greatest enemy was herself. This was civil war perhaps unrivaled even by those of the first century B.C. because much of the fighting and bloodshed took place on Italian soil; there was in addition the very real threat of the break-up of the empire beginning with the Gallic revolt. The cataclysm of the end of the descendants of Augustus, the Julio-Claudian dynasty, each of whom must have felt that he was emperor primarily because of his relation to Augustus, was a real thing. When a century has passed and people have become accustomed to a way of life and form of government, a sudden break will cause a tremendous shock.

Tacitus said early in the work that the secret of empire was out, an emperor could be made anywhere, outside of Rome as well as in the capital; he implied, although he did not state it, that any man could aspire to the principate. In the early days of the republic, the plebeians had had a long and bitter struggle to gain entry to the consulate; now the principate was open to a new man, not only an individual of long-standing nobility but also a *novus homo* in the more traditional sense, a man not representative of ancient nobility whether republican, triumviral, or Augustan. Vespasian was the first new man on the throne of the empire. Coming from the hills north of Rome in the Sabine country, he anticipates the accession within thirty years of the first Roman born in a province, Trajan, the first of a significant series of emperors non-Italian in birth.

Tacitus's great subject is narrated with vividness and detail. The story flows with unparalleled ease and tension. The spacious scope of the subject permits him to introduce an abundance of detail throughout, even on military matters, to such a degree that the old stricture that Tacitus is the most unmilitary of historians can no longer be tolerated. He was, after all, not writing communiqués from the battlefield; he was writing political history and was more concerned with the emotions of men in battle than with the details of battle themselves. Nonetheless, one can follow quite clearly in the *Histories* the details of those battles and can well understand how they were won as well as how they were lost.

The narrative is often treated very dramatically. The author moves from scene to scene and from character to character, interweaving the whole with remarkable skill. The characters themselves are very often tragic in their outlook. They are raised up only to be struck down. Each of them has a *hybris* which, it may be said, is responsible for his end. All have flaws; none is perfect. Only Vespasian of all emperors that Tacitus knew became better after he became emperor. But even he had faults. It is this tremendously psychological treatment of people and, through people, of events that they bring about which gives the *Histories* a flavor unlike that in the shorter works and the *Annals* which were soon to follow.

The *Annals*, too, are incomplete. There survive Books I–IV, the beginning of V, VI, XI (approximately the first third has been lost), and XII to the middle of XVI. In other words, we have four books completely missing in the middle of the work, a large part of one other, a lesser portion of still another, and then the end of the whole from the middle of XVI through probably XVIII. Thus, there is only a little more than half of the original work. The span of years covered by the *Annals* is twice that of the *Histories*, yet the number of books is at most half again as great as that of the *Histories*. Obviously there will be much less detailed coverage. This is no shortcoming, however, because the theme permits treatment in larger units, the emperors did not succeed each other as rapidly as in the beginning of the *Histories*, and Tacitus is concerned not with the survival of the Roman state but rather with the consolidation of the principate after the death of Augustus.

There is only one direct clue to the date of composition in the *Annals* themselves. In II:61, while relating Germanicus's tour of Egypt, Tacitus states that he got as far as Elephantine and Syene, *claustra olim Romani imperii, quod nunc rubrum ad mare patescit*, "formerly the limits of the Roman empire, which now extends to the Red Sea." The crux of the inquiry is the identification of the *rubrum mare*.

If Tacitus means thereby the *sinus Arabicus*, our Red Sea, he must then refer to the establishment of the province of Arabia Nabataea in 105–106, and the composition of Book II will fall in the years soon thereafter. But if *rubrum mare* is to be identified with the western part of the Indian Ocean, a later date is possible. Indeed, the latter interpretation appears more likely. The expression should be understood in the widest sense, the Indian Ocean itself rather than any of its inlets, however important. And the verb *patescit* should be interpreted to refer only to large territories. The only event which would enable Tacitus to write in such terms is Trajan's defeat of the Parthians in 116. It is possible that this contemporary reference was a later insertion into the text, but it is more probable that Tacitus had only recently begun to write and had reached Book II in this year. On this view most of the *Annals* will have been written in the principate of Hadrian.

The beginning of the work sets the tone. There is dissatisfaction with, if not enmity towards, the principate. The pro-oemium is a continuation, in historiographical philosophy, of those of the *Agricola* and the *Histories*. The first three chapters are crucial for understanding Tacitus's frame of reference throughout the entire work. We note that in the first chapter Tacitus telescopes history to reach the present day in about a dozen lines. Vergil, too, had done this in the description of the shield of Aeneas in Book VIII of the *Aeneid* where, from the twins to the battle of Actium, he used less than half his narrative and then devoted the remainder to that culminating struggle of the Roman Revolution. Tacitus here very rapidly mentions the aberrations of government that had occurred in history, aberrations that, precisely because they did not destroy the basic existence of comitial and senatorial sovereignty, are considered as no more than transitory events. But with the establishment of the principate, this of course changed. The principate was an aberration but it did not disappear.

As in the beginning of the *Histories* Tacitus claims objectivity. He did not see any of the Julio-Claudians as a man of mature years; born early in the reign of Nero, he would perhaps have been in his teens when that emperor died. Nonetheless, he finds it compelling to indicate that he will be impartial, and his claim here is stronger than the earlier one. Further, in spite of the fact that he proposes to deal with the empire beginning with the reign of Tiberius, he finds it necessary to set the stage by discoursing briefly on the end of Augustus. In the last sentence of the first chapter, he offers his program, along with his statement of impartiality: *inde consilium mihi pauca de Augusto et extrema tradere, mox Tiberii principatum et cetera, sine ira et studio, quorum causas procul habeo.*

Whether Tacitus was able to achieve his goal of writing history *sine ira et studio,* "without either bitterness or partiality," is one of the most intriguing questions in the study of our historian. What makes Tacitus's stronger claim here more necessary than that in the *Histories* had been is that in this work he is concerned with the basic inquiry into the nature and existence of the principate. It was a form of government which had many admirers and many opponents, with the former far more numerous than the latter but, nonetheless, philosophically the upper class could not be neutral. The principate existed; an individual would have to adjust to it and serve it if one wished a public career. Nevertheless, one did not have to accept it in one's heart and could still believe that the old days had been better.

Tacitus's mood in these three chapters is underscored very strongly by his choice of words such as *exuto,* "cast off," referring to the elimination of Lepidus as a rival to Octavian, and *dominatio,* suggesting autocracy in Augustus's settlement; by innuendo which suggests that people died by treachery and deceit; and by a tone of grudging tribute. At the end of the third chapter there is a very brief statement of the general good health of the empire at the death of the first princeps: *Bellum ea tempestate nullum nisi adversus Germanos supererat, abolendae magis infamiae ob amissum cum Quintilio Varo exercitum quam cupidine proferendi imperii aut dignum ob praemium. domi res tranquillae, eadem magistratuum vocabula; iuniores post Actiacam victoriam, etiam senes plerique inter bella civium nati: quotus quisque reliquus, qui rem publicam vidisset?* "He had no war at the time on his hands except against the Germans, which was rather to wipe out the disgrace of the loss of Quintilius Varus and his army than out of an ambition to extend the empire, or for any adequate recompense. At home all was tranquil, and there were magistrates with the same titles; there was a younger generation, sprung up since the victory of Actium, and even many of the older men had been born during the civil wars. How few were left who had seen the republic!" *Res publica* here can quite appropriately be translated "republic" in the old sense of the free state under the hegemony of the senatorial class. The government which existed now was quite a different thing.

We move then to a presentation of some of the members of the imperial family and to the passing of Augustus. Here too innuendo has full scope, with the intimation that Agrippa Postumus was treacherously murdered, that Augustus had hoped for a reconciliation with his grandson, and that the deed had been accomplished without Tiberius's knowledge.

The sixth chapter begins most ominously: *Primum facinus novi principatus fuit Postumi Agrippae caedes*, "The first crime of the new reign was the murder of Postumus Agrippa." It does not take much imagination to forecast what the rest of Tiberius's reign will be like if this is the beginning. The chapter concludes with the advice of Sallustius Crispus, who had been an intimate of Augustus, to the empress Livia that the Senate must not be allowed to investigate the deed and establish responsibility: *monuit Liviam, ne arcana domus, ne consilia amicorum, ministeria militum vulgarentur, neve Tiberius vim principatus resolveret cuncta ad senatum vocando: eam condicionem esse imperandi, ut non aliter constet quam si uni reddatur.* "He advised Livia not to divulge the secrets of her house or the counsels of friends, or any services performed by the soldiers, nor to let Tiberius weaken the strength of imperial power by referring everything to the Senate, for 'the condition,' he said 'of holding empire is that an account cannot be balanced unless it be rendered to one person.'" In spite of the facade of the restored republic that Augustus had so painfully erected, it was quite obvious that this was an empire governed at the will of one man. This comment is put in the mouth of one of Tacitus's most important minor characters. Sallustius Crispus will appear twice later in the narrative.

To continue, the degradation of the Senate and the upper class in offering allegiance to Tiberius is delineated. Then follows a discussion about the honors to be paid Augustus and comments of the people, both those who favored the first emperor and those who disliked him. Tacitus here displays virtuosity in the treatment of material. The favorable report of Augustus comes first and is much briefer than the opposing opinions. The net effect is that one believes and remembers the ill. Many, indeed most, of the criticisms levelled at the first emperor concern his private household and events which marked the triumviral period. No one, not even Augustus himself, would have been able to excuse them absolutely; but the dividing line between the young Octavian and the mature Augustus, who reigned after the battle of Actium for some forty-five years, was totally blurred so that the ill-doings of the early years overwhelm the achievements of the later ones.

Tiberius's succession then follows with his perhaps insincere attempt to resist the empire when he already in fact possessed and exercised its prime features, the tribunician power and the *imperium*, and several rivals are mentioned. Tacitus introduces these men, it may be, for little reason other than to have an opportunity early in the work to present the importance of the capacity of being emperor. Tiberius himself claims that only the mind of the deified Augustus had been equal to such a crushing burden (1:11,1): *solam divi Augusti mentem tantae molis capacem.* What Tacitus mentioned in the obituary of Galba, *capax imperii*, is a theme that pervades much of his historical work, although he does not himself use the word very often. Of the rivals who are mentioned by Augustus, there were three: a man who was *capax* but who did not long for the purple; another who was greedy for it but *minor*, precisely the opposite of *capax;* a third who was by no means unworthy and a likely challenger if opportunity should offer. It may not be too much to see throughout Tacitus's work a yearning to underscore those who, given the chance, would have served the empire well, the few men in the span of one hundred years who were indeed *capaces imperii.*

From this beginning (the first fifteen chapters which set the scene in Rome and in the imperial house and, perhaps most importantly, carry us through the death of the first emperor to the accession of the second) Tacitus turns to affairs that are basically foreign without, however, totally ignoring events at Rome, particularly to emphasize the renewed importance of the laws against treason, *maiestas*, the significance of which will be a major subject of later books. Tacitus's narrative has both a hero and an antihero in the first three books. As soon as Tacitus reaches the beginning of chapter sixteen, he sets the tone: *Hic rerum urbanarum status erat, cum Pannonicas legiones seditio incessit, nullis novis causis, nisi quod mutatus princeps licentiam turbarum et ex civili bello spem praemiorum ostendebat.* "This was the state of affairs at Rome when a mutiny broke out in the legions of Pannonia, which could be traced to no fresh cause except the change of emperors and the prospect it held out of license in tumult and of profit from a civil war." We are treated in rapid succession to the uprising of the Pannonian legions and those of the armies of Germany and the attempt to quell them by the emperor's sons, more precisely his own son Drusus in Pannonia and his adopted son Germanicus, his natural nephew, in Germany. Drusus receives much less attention than does Germanicus throughout the work, but he is nonetheless presented here as the more successful of the two. Once the mutiny in Germany is ended, Germanicus undertakes a campaign against the Germans. We are brought to the site of the Teutoburg Forest where in the year A.D. 9 the German Arminius had destroyed three legions with their commander Quintilius Varus. There are vivid scenes of war and battle; Germanicus's enterprises are immediately successful, but their long-range effect is minimal.

In the second book, there is a tremendously vivid representation of the storm in which Tacitus describes Germanicus's almost fatal miscalculations (23–24), and where Tacitus may have had recourse to first-hand reports of what happened, particularly the poem of an officer of Germanicus, Albinovanus Pedo, as well as the grand scene in the first book of the *Aeneid.*

When, however, summer was at its height, some of the legions were sent back overland into winter-quarters, but most of them Caesar put on board the fleet and brought down the river Amisia to the ocean. At first the calm waters merely sounded with the oars of a thousand vessels or were ruffled by the sailing ships. Soon, a hailstorm bursting from a black mass of clouds, while the waves rolled hither and thither under tempestuous gales from every quarter, rendered clear sight impossible, and the steering difficult, while our soldiers, terrorstricken and without any experience of disasters on the sea, by embarrassing the sailors or giving them clumsy aid, neutralized the services of the skilled crews. After a while, wind and wave shifted wholly to the south, and from the hilly lands and deep rivers of Germany came, with a huge line of rolling clouds, a strong blast, all the more frightful from the frozen north which was so near to them, and instantly caught and drove the ships hither and thither into the open ocean, or on islands with steep cliffs or which hidden shoals made perilous. These they just escaped, with difficulty, and when the tide changed and bore them the same way as the wind, they could not hold to their anchors or bale out the water which rushed in upon them. Horses, beasts of burden, baggage, were thrown overboard, in order to lighten the hulls which leaked copiously through their sides, while the waves too dashed over them.

As the ocean is stormier than all other seas, and as Germany is conspicuous for the terrors of its climate, so in novelty and extent did this disaster transcend every other, for all around were hostile coasts, or an expanse so vast and deep that it is thought to be the remotest shoreless sea. Some of the vessels were swallowed up; many were wrecked on distant islands, and the soldiers, finding there no form of human life, perished of hunger, except some who supported existence on carcases of horses washed on the same shores. Germanicus's trireme alone reached the country of the Chauci. Day and night, on those rocks and promontories he would incessantly exclaim that he was himself responsible for this awful ruin, and friends scarce restrained him from seeking death in the same sea.

At last, as the tide ebbed and the wind blew favourably, the shattered vessels with but few rowers, or clothing spread as sails, some towed by the more powerful, returned, and Germanicus, having speedily repaired them, sent them to search the islands. Many by that means were recovered. The Angrivarii, who had lately been admitted to our alliance, re-

stored to us several whom they had ransomed from the in-
land tribes. Some had been carried to Britain and were sent
back by the petty chiefs. Every one, as he returned from some
far-distant region, told of wonders, of violent hurricanes,
and unknown birds, of monsters of the sea, of forms half-
human, half-beastlike, things they had really seen or in their
terror believed.

Germanicus is then recalled, with high honor, but it is
thought Tiberius is jealous of his success. Innuendo may be
at work here, but the reason given for the recall is that his
talents are needed in the East against the threat of the Parthians. On his way thither he undertakes a grand tour of in-
spection of many cities, among them Athens, visits Egypt
without permission, thereby violating the long-standing stip-
ulations of Augustus and enraging Tiberius, and at last arrives
in Syria, now governed by a man who is a bitter personal
enemy of his but an extremely close confidant of the emperor.
This is Gnaeus Piso, and the last part of Book II is concerned
with the rivalry of these two important men. Their conflict
ends with Germanicus's death. He himself suspected murder
at the hands of Piso and charges his wife and followers to
beware of Piso and to bring him to justice.

The first part of Book III is concerned with the trial of Piso
and his suicide when he realizes that the emperor is incapable
of supporting him or unwilling to do so. The emotional level
is extremely high throughout, for the atmosphere is charged
not only with the investigation of a crime alleged to have removed the heir of empire and the favorite of the Roman
people, but also with the fierce nature and thirst for revenge
of Agrippina, the widow, and the belief that the deed had
been accomplished at the instance of the emperor and his
mother. Indeed Tacitus suggests as much when, in a rare
intrusion of his own person into the narrative, he reports
(16,1), "I remember to have heard old men say that a docu-
ment was often seen in Piso's hands, the substance of which
he never himself divulged, but which his friends repeatedly
declared contained a letter from Tiberius with instructions
referring to Germanicus, and that it was his intention to produce it before the Senate and upbraid the emperor, had he not

been deluded by vain promises from Sejanus. Nor did he perish, they said, by his own hand, but by that of one sent to be his executioner. Neither of these statements would I positively affirm; still it would not have been right for me to conceal what was related by those who lived up to the time of my youth." The remainder of the book deals with a medley of subjects, tying up many of the important aspects of Tiberius's first nine years as emperor.

Book IV begins with the detailed introduction of the man who can be called the evil spirit of the Tiberian years, Lucius Aelius Sejanus, the prefect of the praetorian guard to whom, in the first chapter, Tacitus gives a Sallustian biography. He is very much like Catiline in ability, in ambition, and in failings, and it is surely part of Tacitus's purpose to make his readers realize what the end is likely to be.

The first seven chapters of this book present a review of the empire, and it is quite remarkable that almost everything that is said is complimentary and good. The empire was on an even keel, the laws were enforced impartially, the emperor himself behaved in an unexceptionable manner. Yet in the year 23 all this changed. Chiefly responsible was Sejanus, whose sudden ascendency was a sign that the fortune of the empire was becoming capricious: *cum repente turbare fortuna coepit* (1,1). The world became disjointed.

In chapter seven Tacitus bluntly states that it was in this year that Tiberius began to change for the worse; and it was the death of Drusus, his son, and not that of Germanicus which was responsible for this change. This is a very important point in the understanding of Tacitus's history. The other ancient sources for these events, Suetonius and Dio Cassius, agree in placing the turning point of Tiberius's reign in the year 19, precisely with the death of Germanicus. The source from which these two drew must have read this way. Tacitus, either because he followed a different source or because his own judgment led him to this conclusion, chose rather to put the blame not on Germanicus's death but on the meteoric rise of the evil minister Sejanus, whose first crime was the murder of Drusus.

The second half of the first hexad of the *Annals* is marked by the constant interplay of three strong characters—Tiberius, Sejanus, and Agrippina, Germanicus's widow—and the contest between the latter pair to maintain or obtain influence over the emperor. Sejanus gradually won Tiberius's complete confidence, a process culminating in his total disregard for his own safety in protecting the emperor's person at Spelunca, the modern Sperlonga, when an artificial grotto in which the emperor was dining began to collapse (IV:59). It was at Sejanus's behest that Tiberius removed himself from Rome, first to Campania and then to Capri. Never, for more than a decade, did he return to the capital, while Sejanus, for the first five years of this period, himself ran the government in Rome.

Book V, which is largely missing, would have detailed the fall of Sejanus. We do not possess what must have been one of Tacitus's most vivid narratives. We can get a sense of its matter from Juvenal, who speaks of a long letter coming from Capri which was read to the Senate; at the end Sejanus was condemned and at once put to death, his statues overturned, and his body thrown into the Tiber. Book VI continues with what Tacitus represents as a blood bath, with the slaughter of the supporters of Sejanus, and Tiberius's own personal disintegration until, at the end of life, he was no more than a monster satisfying his cruelest whims.

The sixth book concludes with a detailed obituary and character sketch. The last chapter makes it very clear that Tacitus considered Tiberius's character to have always been monstrous.

> Pater ei Nero et utrimque origo gentis Claudiae, quamquam mater in Liviam et mox Iuliam familiam adoptionibus transierit. casus prima ab infantia ancipites; nam proscriptum patrem exsul secutus, ubi domum Augusti privignus introiit, multis aemulis conflictatus est, dum Marcellus et Agrippa, mox Gaius Luciusque Caesares viguere; etiam frater eius Drusus prosperiore civium amore erat. sed maxime in lubrico egit accepta in matrimonium Iulia, impudicitiam uxoris tolerans aut declinans. dein Rhodo regressus vacuos principis penates duodecim annis, mox rei Romanae arbitrium tribus ferme et viginti obtinuit. morum quoque tempora illi diversa: egregium vita famaque, quoad privatus vel in imperiis

sub Augusto fuit; occultum ac subdolum fingendis virtuti-
bus, donec Germanicus ac Drusus superfuere; idem inter
bona malaque mixtus incolumi matre; intestabilis saevitia,
sed obtectis libidinibus, dum Seianum dilexit timuitve: pos-
tremo in scelera simul ac dedecora prorupit, postquam re-
moto pudore et metu suo tantum ingenio utebatur.

Nero was his father, and he was on both sides descended
from the Claudian house, though his mother passed by adoption, first into the Livian, then into the Julian family. From
earliest infancy, perilous vicissitudes were his lot. Himself an
exile, he was the companion of a proscribed father, and on
being admitted as a stepson into the house of Augustus, he
had to struggle with many rivals, so long as Marcellus and
Agrippa and, subsequently, Caius and Lucius Caesar were in
their glory. Again his brother Drusus enjoyed in a greater
degree the affection of the citizens. But he was more than
ever on dangerous ground after his marriage with Julia,
whether he tolerated or escaped from his wife's profligacy.
On his return from Rhodes he ruled the emperor's now heir-
less house for twelve years, and the Roman world, with absolute sway, for about twenty-three. His character too had its
distinct periods. It was a bright time in his life and reputation,
while under Augustus he was a private citizen or held high
offices; a time of reserve and crafty assumption of virtue, as
long as Germanicus and Drusus were alive. Again, while his
mother lived, he was a compound of good and evil; he was
infamous for his cruelty, though he veiled his debaucheries,
while he loved or feared Sejanus. Finally, he plunged into
every wickedness and disgrace, when fear and shame being
cast off, he simply indulged his own inclinations.

In his earlier years, Tiberius disguised his true nature under
the influence of first one person and then another; then, when
the last restraining influence had been removed, he allowed
his real self to appear. Not everyone will accept this kind of
judgment, but it must be remembered that in antiquity the
general understanding of an individual's character, his *ingenium*, was that he was born with it and that it never changed
or developed. Therefore, if there were different phases of a
person's character during his life, there must be an explanation; dissimulation is the easiest answer.

The kind of reign that Gaius had was accurately forecast by Tacitus in VI:48, 1–3, in the final words of a great man, Lucius Arruntius:

sibi satis aetatis, neque aliud paenitendum quam quod inter ludibria et pericula anxiam senectam toleravisset, diu Seiano, nunc Macroni, semper alicui potentium invisus, non culpa, sed ut flagitiorum impatiens. sane paucos ad suprema principis dies posse vitari: quem ad modum evasurum imminentis iuventam? an, cum Tiberius post tantam rerum experientiam vi dominationis convulsus et mutatus sit, C. Caesarem vix finita pueritia, ignarum omnium aut pessimis innutritum, meliora capessiturum Macrone duce, qui ut deterior ad opprimendum Seianum delectus plura per scelera rem publicam conflictavisset? prospectare iam se acrius servitium, eoque fugere simul acta et instantia. haec vatis in modum dictitans venas resolvit. documento sequentia erunt bene Arruntium morte usum.

"He had had enough of life, and all he regretted was that he had endured amid scorn and peril an old age of anxious fears, long detested by Sejanus, now by Macro, always, indeed, by some powerful minister, not for any fault, but as a man who could not tolerate gross iniquities. Granted the possibility of passing safely through the few last days of Tiberius. How was he to be secure under the youth of the coming sovereign? Was it probable that, when Tiberius with his long experience of affairs was, under the influence of absolute power, wholly perverted and changed, Caius Caesar, who had hardly completed his boyhood, was thoroughly ignorant and bred under the vilest training, would enter on a better course, with Macro for his guide, who having been selected for his superior wickedness to crush Sejanus, had by yet more numerous crimes been the scourge of the State? He now foresaw a still more galling slavery, and therefore sought to flee alike from the past and from the impending future." While he thus spoke like a prophet, he opened his veins. What followed will be a proof that Arruntius rightly chose death.

Gaius, too, will have his evil spirit in the person of Macro.

This narrative resumes in Book XI. The entire principate of Gaius and the first six years of Claudius have disappeared. In Books XI and XII, the picture of the emperor Claudius as a buffoon, as a man ill chosen for the empire (whose only recommendation was his relation to the first princeps and the fact that he was Germanicus's brother), and as the plaything of his freedmen and his wives, is a very coherent one. Yet Tacitus too makes it quite obvious that Claudius was much more than this. He was an administrator with remarkable talent and assiduity; this is most easily understood in the speech that Claudius made on the admission of certain Gallic chieftains to the Senate. We have a large part of Claudius's original address preserved on a bronze tablet found at Lyons in France. This is the only opportunity moderns have in the entire realm of ancient history to compare an original text with the version that a historian later produced. Claudius's speech is far more rambling, far more imprecise. Tacitus has tightened it up and underscored his arguments in a much more effective way. He has not done the original a disservice, nor has he misrepresented it; he has, on the contrary, made it clear that Claudius's administrative talents and historical sense were by no means negligible. This conclusion is supported by another speech that Claudius delivered, of which there is no version in the text, on the status of the Anauni, a people who lived in the Alps and suddenly found their citizenship challenged.

Book XIII begins with ominous tones, recalling the beginning of Tiberius's reign, the sixth chapter of the first book: *prima novo principatu mors Iunii Silani proconsulis Asiae.* "The first death under the new emperor, that of Junius Silanus, proconsul of Asia." It takes little imagination to anticipate that this will be the mood of Nero's entire principate. Barely a young man, he starts out fairly well because of the excellent tutors and guides that his mother had chosen for him: Seneca, the philosopher, and Burrus, the commander of the praetorian guard. Nonetheless, the seeds for evil are present in Nero and are visible throughout; bit by bit, as the narrative proceeds, they take root and flourish. First Britannicus is murdered; soon thereafter follows Agrippina, with some of Tacitus's most remarkable narrative ability brought to bear at the beginning of Book XIV. Octavia is then eliminated; the aristocracy, in the persons of some of its most prestigious members, prepares a conspiracy against the emperor. It does not succeed, but during it the soldier Subrius bluntly tells the emperor to his face why he has taken up arms against him (xv:67):

> Shortly afterwards, the information of the same men proved fatal to Subrius Flavus. At first he grounded his defence on his moral contrast to the others, implying that an armed soldier, like himself, would never have shared such an attempt with unarmed and effeminate associates. Then, when he was pressed, he embraced the glory of a full confession. Questioned by Nero as to the motives which had led him on to forget his oath of allegiance, "I hated you," he replied; "yet not a soldier was more loyal to you while you deserved to be loved. I began to hate you when you became the murderer of your mother and your wife, a charioteer, an actor, and an incendiary." I have given the man's very words, because they were not, like those of Seneca, generally published, though the rough and vigorous sentiments of a soldier ought to be no less known.
>
> Throughout the conspiracy nothing, it was certain, fell with more terror on the ears of Nero, who was as unused to be told of the crimes he perpetrated as he was eager in their perpetration. The punishment of Flavus was intrusted to Veianius Niger, a tribune. At his direction, a pit was dug in a neighbouring field. Flavus, on seeing it, censured it as too shallow and confined, saying to the soldiers around him, "Even this is not according to military rule." When bidden to offer his neck resolutely, "I wish," said he, "that your stroke may be as resolute." The tribune trembled greatly, and having only just severed his head at two blows, vaunted his brutality to Nero, saying that he had slain him with a blow and a half.

The work ends with the trial of Thrasea Paetus and the suicide of the great philosopher and statesman.

There are two high points in these last books from the point of view of historical virtuosity. One we have already mentioned, the murder of Agrippina, which deserves presentation in full, for its brilliant evocation of mood and emotion (xiv: 1–8).

> In the year of the consulship of Caius Vipstanus and Caius Fonteius, Nero deferred no more a long meditated

crime. Length of power had matured his daring, and his passion for Poppaea daily grew more ardent. As the woman had no hope of marriage for herself or of Octavia's divorce while Agrippina lived, she would reproach the emperor with incessant vituperation and sometimes call him in jest a mere ward who was under the rule of others, and was so far from having empire that he had not even his liberty. "Why," she asked, "was her marriage put off? Was it, forsooth, her beauty and her ancestors, with their triumphal honours, that failed to please, or her being a mother, and her sincere heart? No; the fear was that as a wife at least she would divulge the wrongs of the Senate, and the wrath of the people at the arrogance and rapacity of his mother. If the only daughter-in-law Agrippina could bear was one who wished evil to her son, let her be restored to her union with Otho. She would go anywhere in the world, where she might hear of the insults heaped on the emperor, rather than witness them, and be also involved in his perils."

These and the like complaints, rendered impressive by tears and by the cunning of an adulteress, no one checked, as all longed to see the mother's power broken, while not a person believed that the son's hatred would steel his heart to her murder.

Cluvius relates that Agrippina in her eagerness to retain her influence went so far that more than once at midday, when Nero, even at that hour, was flushed with wine and feasting, she presented herself attractively attired to her half intoxicated son and offered him her person, and that when kinsfolk observed wanton kisses and caresses, portending infamy, it was Seneca who sought a female's aid against a woman's fascinations, and hurried in Acte, the freed-girl, who alarmed at her own peril and at Nero's disgrace, told him that the incest was notorious, as his mother boasted of it, and that the soldiers would never endure the rule of an impious sovereign. Fabius Rusticus tells us that it was not Agrippina, but Nero, who lusted for the crime, and that it was frustrated by the adroitness of that same freed-girl. Cluvius's account, however, is also that of all other authors, and popular belief inclines to it, whether it was that Agrippina really conceived such a monstrous wickedness in her heart, or perhaps because the thought of a strange passion seemed comparatively credible in a woman, who in her girlish years had allowed herself to be seduced by Lepidus in the hope of winning power, had stooped with a like ambition to the lust of Pallas, and had trained herself for every infamy by her marriage with her uncle.

Nero accordingly avoided secret interviews with her, and when she withdrew to her gardens or to her estates at Tusculum and Antium, he praised her for courting repose. At last, convinced that she would be too formidable, wherever she might dwell, he resolved to destroy her, merely deliberating whether it was to be accomplished by poison, or by the sword, or by any other violent means. Poison at first seemed best, but, were it to be administered at the imperial table, the result could not be referred to chance after the recent circumstances of the death of Britannicus. Again, to tamper with the servants of a woman who, from her familiarity with crime, was on her guard against treachery, appeared to be extremely difficult, and then, too, she had fortified her constitution by the use of antidotes. How again the dagger and its work were to be kept secret, no one could suggest, and it was feared too that whoever might be chosen to execute such a crime would spurn the order.

An ingenious suggestion was offered by Anicetus, a freedman, commander of the fleet at Misenum, who had been tutor to Nero in boyhood and had a hatred of Agrippina which she reciprocated. He explained that a vessel could be constructed, from which a part might by a contrivance be detached, when out at sea, so as to plunge her unawares into the water. "Nothing," he said, "allowed of accidents so much as the sea, and should she be overtaken by shipwreck, who would be so unfair as to impute to crime an offence committed by the winds and waves? The emperor would add the honour of a temple and of shrines to the deceased lady, with every other display of filial affection."

Nero liked the device, favoured as it also was by the particular time, for he was celebrating Minerva's five days' festival at Baiae. Thither he enticed his mother by repeated assurances that children ought to bear with the irritability of parents and to soothe their tempers, wishing thus to spread a rumour of reconciliation and to secure Agrippina's acceptance through the feminine credulity, which easily believes what gives joy. As she approached, he went to the shore to meet her (she was coming from Antium), welcomed her with outstretched hand and embrace, and conducted her to

Bauli. This was the name of a country house, washed by a bay of the sea, between the promontory of Misenum and the lake of Baiae. Here was a vessel distinguished from others by its equipment, seemingly meant, among other things, to do honour to his mother; for she had been accustomed to sail in a trireme, with a crew of marines. And now she was invited to a banquet, that night might serve to conceal the crime. It was well known that somebody had been found to betray it, that Agrippina had heard of the plot, and in doubt whether she was to believe it, was conveyed to Baiae in her litter. There some soothing words allayed her fear; she was graciously received, and seated at table above the emperor. Nero prolonged the banquet with various conversation, passing from a youth's playful familiarity to an air of constraint, which seemed to indicate serious thought, and then, after protracted festivity, escorted her on her departure, clinging with kisses to her eyes and bosom, either to crown his hypocrisy or because the last sight of a mother on the eve of destruction caused a lingering even in that brutal heart.

A night of brilliant starlight with the calm of a tranquil sea was granted by heaven, seemingly, to convict the crime. The vessel had not gone far, Agrippina having with her two of her intimate attendants, one of whom, Crepereius Gallus, stood near the helm, while Acerronia, reclining at Agrippina's feet as she reposed herself, spoke joyfully of her son's repentance and of the recovery of the mother's influence, when at a given signal the ceiling of the place, which was loaded with a quantity of lead, fell in, and Crepereius was crushed and instantly killed. Agrippina and Acerronia were protected by the projecting sides of the couch, which happened to be too strong to yield under the weight. But this was not followed by the breaking up of the vessel; for all were bewildered, and those too, who were in the plot, were hindered by the unconscious majority. The crew then thought it best to throw the vessel on one side and so sink it, but they could not themselves promptly unite to face the emergency, and others, by counteracting the attempt, gave an opportunity of a gentler fall into the sea. Acerronia, however, thoughtlessly exclaiming that she was Agrippina, and imploring help for the emperor's mother, was despatched with poles and oars, and such naval implements as chance offered. Agrippina was silent and was thus the less recognized;

still, she received a wound in her shoulder. She swam, then met with some small boats which conveyed her to the Lucrine lake, and so entered her house.

There she reflected how for this very purpose she had been invited by a lying letter and treated with conspicuous honour, how also it was near the shore, not from being driven by winds or dashed on rocks, that the vessel had in its upper part collapsed, like a mechanism anything but nautical. She pondered too the death of Acerronia; she looked at her own wound, and saw that her only safeguard against treachery was to ignore it. Then she sent her freedman Agerinus to tell her son how by heaven's favour and his good fortune she had escaped a terrible disaster; that she begged him, alarmed, as he might be, by his mother's peril, to put off the duty of a visit, as for the present she needed repose. Meanwhile, pretending that she felt secure, she applied remedies to her wound, and fomentations to her person. She then ordered search to be made for the will of Acerronia, and her property to be sealed, in this alone throwing off disguise.

Nero, meantime, as he waited for tidings of the consummation of the deed, received information that she had escaped with the injury of a slight wound, after having so far encountered the peril that there could be no question as to its author. Then, paralysed with terror and protesting that she would show herself the next moment eager for vengeance, either arming the slaves or stirring up the soldiery, or hastening to the Senate and the people, to charge him with the wreck, with her wound, and with the destruction of her friends, he asked what resource he had against all this, unless something could be at once devised by Burrus and Seneca. He had instantly summoned both of them, and possibly they were already in the secret. There was a long silence on their part; they feared they might remonstrate in vain, or believed the crisis to be such that Nero must perish, unless Agrippina were at once crushed. Thereupon Seneca was so far the more prompt as to glance back on Burrus, as if to ask him whether the bloody deed must be required of the soldiers. Burrus replied "that the praetorians were attached to the whole family of the Caesars, and remembering Germanicus would not dare a savage deed on his offspring. It was for Anicetus to accomplish his promise."

Anicetus, without a pause, claimed for himself the consummation of the crime. At those words, Nero declared that that day gave him empire, and that a freedman was the author of this mighty boon. "Go," he said, "with all speed and take with you the men readiest to execute your orders." He himself, when he had heard of the arrival of Agrippina's messenger, Agerinus, contrived a theatrical mode of accusation, and, while the man was repeating his message, threw down a sword at his feet, then ordered him to be put in irons, as a detected criminal, so that he might invent a story how his mother had plotted the emperor's destruction and in the shame of discovered guilt had by her own choice sought death.

Meantime, Agrippina's peril being universally known and taken to be an accidental occurrence, everybody, the moment he heard of it, hurried down to the beach. Some climbed projecting piers; some the nearest vessels; others, as far as their stature allowed, went into the sea; some, again, stood with outstretched arms, while the whole shore rung with wailings, with prayers and cries, as different questions were asked and uncertain answers given. A vast multitude streamed to the spot with torches, and as soon as all knew that she was safe, they at once prepared to wish her joy, till the sight of an armed and threatening force scared them away. Anicetus then surrounded the house with a guard, and having burst open the gates, dragged off the slaves who met him, till he came to the door of her chamber, where a few still stood, after the rest had fled in terror at the attack. A small lamp was in the room, and one slave-girl with Agrippina, who grew more and more anxious, as no messenger came from her son, not even Agerinus, while the appearance of the shore was changed, a solitude one moment, then sudden bustle and tokens of the worst catastrophe. As the girl rose to depart, she exclaimed, "Do you too forsake me?" and looking round saw Anicetus, who had with him the captain of the trireme, Herculeius, and Obaritus, a centurion of marines. "If," said she, "you have come to see me, take back word that I have recovered, but if you are here to do a crime, I believe nothing about my son; he has not ordered his mother's murder."

The assassins closed in round her couch, and the captain of the trireme first struck her head violently with a club.

Then, as the centurion bared his sword for the fatal deed, presenting her person, she exclaimed, "Smite my womb," and with many wounds she was slain.

The other is the fire at Rome and the ensuing persecution (if that is the proper word) of the Christians, with the hatred that Nero won for himself by suspicion for the first act and the indignation against his policy roused by the second. These are treated in XV:38 and 44 although the intervening chapters are important as well.

A disaster followed, whether accidental or treacherously contrived by the emperor, is uncertain, as authors have given both accounts, worse, however, and more dreadful than any which have ever happened to this city by the violence of fire. It had its beginning in that part of the circus which adjoins the Palatine and Caelian hills, where, amid the shops containing inflammable wares, the conflagration both broke out and instantly became so fierce and so rapid from the wind that it seized in its grasp the entire length of the circus. For here there were no houses fenced in by solid masonry, or temples surrounded by walls, or any other obstacle to interpose delay. The blaze in its fury ran first through the level portions of the city, then rising to the hills, while it again devastated every place below them, it outstripped all preventive measures; so rapid was the mischief and so completely at its mercy the city, with those narrow winding passages and irregular streets, which characterised old Rome. Added to this were the wailings of terror-stricken women, the feebleness of age, the helpless inexperience of childhood, the crowds who sought to save themselves or others, dragging out the infirm or waiting for them, and by their hurry in the one case, by their delay in the other, aggravating the confusion. Often, while they looked behind them, they were intercepted by flames on their side or in their face. Or if they reached a refuge close at hand, when this too was seized by the fire, they found that even places which they had imagined to be remote, were involved in the same calamity. At last, doubting what they should avoid or whither betake themselves, they crowded the streets or flung themselves down in the fields, while some who had lost their all, even their very daily bread, and others out of love for their kinsfolk, whom they had been unable to rescue, perished, though escape was open to them. And no one dared to stop the mischief, because of incessant menaces from a number of persons who forbade the extinguishing of the flames, because again others openly hurled brands, and kept shouting that there was one who gave them authority, either seeking to plunder more freely, or obeying orders. . . .

Such indeed were the precautions of human wisdom. The next thing was to seek means of propitiating the gods, and recourse was had to the Sibylline books, by the direction of which prayers were offered to Vulcanus, Ceres, and Proserpina. Juno, too, was entreated by the matrons, first, in the Capitol, then on the nearest part of the coast, whence water was procured to sprinkle the fane and image of the goddess. And there were sacred banquets and nightly vigils celebrated by married women. But all human efforts, all the lavish gifts of the emperor, and the propitiations of the gods, did not banish the sinister belief that the conflagration was the result of an order. Consequently, to get rid of the report, Nero fastened the guilt and inflicted the most exquisite tortures on a class hated for their abominations, called Christians by the populace. Christus, from whom the name had its origin, suffered the extreme penalty during the reign of Tiberius at the hands of one of our procurators, Pontius Pilatus, and a most mischievous superstition, thus checked for the moment, again broke out not only in Judaea, the first source of the evil, but even in Rome, where all things hideous and shameful from every part of the world find their centre and become popular. Accordingly, an arrest was first made of all who pleaded guilty; then, upon their information, an immense multitude was convicted, not so much of the crime of firing the city, as of hatred against mankind. Mockery of every sort was added to their deaths. Covered with the skins of beasts, they were torn by dogs and perished, or were nailed to crosses, or were doomed to the flames and burnt, to serve as a nightly illumination, when daylight had expired.

Nero offered his gardens for the spectacle, and was exhibiting a show in the circus, while he mingled with the people in the dress of a charioteer or stood aloft on a car. Hence, even for criminals who deserved extreme and exemplary punishment, there arose a feeling of compassion;

for it was not, as it seemed, for the public good, but to glut one man's cruelty, that they were being destroyed.

Throughout the entire *Annals*, as they have survived, we see a master historian at work. His approach is largely annalistic; he generally deals with events chronologically but occasionally goes beyond the bounds of strict chronology to treat a theme coherently. This is particularly the case in the later books when, detailing the wars of Corbulo against the Parthians, he permits events to embrace more than one year. He brilliantly molds his mood by choice of vocabulary, by skillful positioning of events and commentary upon them, and by repetition of suggestion. A splendid instance of the last is the treatment of Sallustius Crispus, who was responsible, it was said in Book I, for the murder of Agrippa Postumus, whoever it was who gave the orders; in Book II he is called upon to accomplish the same kind of task, the elimination of an imposter who claimed to be Agrippa Postumus. Lastly, when Sallustius himself died, Tacitus gives him a splendid obituary, which leaves no doubt but that he had been responsible for the original murder (III:30):

> Crispus was of equestrian descent and grandson of a sister of Caius Sallustius, that most admirable Roman historian, by whom he was adopted and whose name he took. Though his road to preferment was easy, he chose to emulate Maecenas, and without rising to a senator's rank, he surpassed in power many who had won triumphs and consulships. He was a contrast to the manners of antiquity in his elegance and refinement, and in the sumptuousness of his wealth he was almost a voluptuary. But beneath all this was a vigorous mind, equal to the greatest labours, the more active in proportion as he made a show of sloth and apathy. And so while Maecenas lived, he stood next in favour to him, and was afterwards the chief depository of imperial secrets, and accessory to the murder of Postumus Agrippa, till in advanced age he retained the shadow rather than the substance of the emperor's friendship. The same too had happened to Maecenas, so rarely is it the destiny of power to be lasting, or perhaps a sense of weariness steals over princes when they have bestowed everything, or over favourites, when there is nothing left them to desire.

Further, this obituary enables Tacitus to comment upon the transitory nature of influence with an emperor by introducing comparison with Maecenas.

Tacitus accomplishes this mood by his style and by his suggestion of necessity, that things had to happen as they ultimately did, although of course this was by no means always the case. His Latin in the first six books is extremely tight and contorted—one might almost say unnatural. He goes far beyond Sallust, his master, in the desire for a poetical vocabulary, to emphasize inconcinnity, always to surprise the reader.

The last six books are by no means as vigorous on this score, perhaps because the subject does not call for it. When dealing with Tiberius, a historian has a subject worthy of genius. What was his character? Why did he act as he did? Was he always the same kind of man? With Claudius and Nero, their true natures were fairly obvious, and there was need only for a simple narrative. The Latin of these books, therefore, is much simpler. We must not, however, claim a return to Ciceronian standard, for this is not the case.

These two works, the *Histories* and the *Annals*, are perhaps the greatest achievement of Latin historiography. They display an insight into the minds of men, into the workings of government, into the power politics of an empire, that are unrivaled by either Sallust or Livy. The only ancient author who can match Tacitus is Thucydides. It would be interesting to know what Quintilian's judgment would have been when, in the tenth book of his *Institutio oratoria*, he paired historians, linking Livy with Herodotus and Sallust with Thucydides. Had Quintilian written some twenty years later, he would surely have replaced Sallust with a man who was perhaps his former student who, he would have been dismayed to realize, had gone far beyond the career that he had originally pursued, and had developed a style unlike that which Quintilian considered perfect and most eminent, that of Cicero. Beyond question Tacitus would have been ranked as foremost of Rome's historians.

V. SOURCES AND ANTECEDENTS

The historical literature of the first century A.D. is a large void. We have only the skimpiest and most meager fragments of most of the writers who preceded Tacitus, and in some instances know little more than names.

The greatest of his masters, if we may use the word, were Sallust and Livy, both of whom he speaks of admiringly. In *Agricola* 10,3, he calls Livy, in conjunction with Fabius Rusticus, an *eloquentissimus auctor*, "a very polished writer," and in *Annals* III: 30,2, Sallust is judged *rerum Romanarum florentissimus auctor*, "that most admirable Roman historian." Tacitus's favor focused most particularly on Sallust. His themes, his keen insight into the collapse of a people and an empire, his historical approach with its emphasis upon characterization, his language with its tendency toward archaism, his style with its great speed and urgency, the renowned *velocitas*, all attracted Tacitus. Obviously, since the period which Sallust treated was much earlier than his own, there could be no direct use of Sallust for source material. Yet trains of thought and suggestions for treatment of subject produce an affinity that is no less great.

The debt to Livy is not so easy to discern, for the Augustan books, whose subject would have been congenial to Tacitus, have disappeared. Livy is a splendid stylist and a serious historian, *eloquentiae ac fidei praeclarus in primis* (*Ann.* IV:34,3), but his language and style are mild and mellow, marked by a "milky richness," *lactea ubertas,* as Quintilian put it. That was not good enough for Tacitus, who needed something more astringent. He must have had some lack of regard for Livy's naiveté; but the subject, the history of the imperial Roman people, certainly attracted him, and there are places, although by no means as numerous as in Sallust, where one can assume that Livy served as Tacitus's source, either directly or to obtain opposite effects.

The one complete work covering the early principate as part of its subject is the *Roman History* of Velleius Paterculus. Little more than a compendium of the early days of Rome, the detail and scope increase markedly as he approached his own day. A soldier who had served under Tiberius, he was an enthusiastic (some might say uncritical) adherent and admirer of the second emperor as well as of the founder of the principate. The work covered more than half of Tiberius's reign, to the year 29 or 30. The downfall of Sejanus would have embarrassed Velleius, assuming that the latter had died before that event; he would have had to find a way to implicate in treason a great minister whom before he had abundantly praised. Velleius's history was unquestionably known to Tacitus, but he never alludes to it, nor does he mention his predecessor. Suffect consuls in the years 60 and 61 were probably his sons; had Tacitus so desired, he could well have introduced comment about their father in such a context. But his complete silence leads to the conclusion that Tacitus had no regard for Velleius's work and that he did not use it as a source. He obviously found it too lacking in depth and insight for his own purposes.

The most immediate sources, therefore, are those that are largely gone. We know the names of some half dozen who wrote of the imperial events of the period which Tacitus himself covered. He cites these sparingly, but more frequently he refers to anonymous sources, whom he designates by words such as *plerique,* "several"; at least we know that he is making use of material that he has researched. Under these circumstances, perhaps it will be easiest to mention briefly the various authors to whom Tacitus refers.

Quintilian (*Inst. or.* X:1,102–104) joins in praise the names of Servilius Nonianus and Aufidius Bassus: (*Servilius*) *et ipse a nobis auditus est, clari vir ingenii et sententiis creber, sed minus pressus quam historiae auctoritas postulat. Quam paulum aetate praecedens eum Bassus Aufidius egregie, utique in libris belli Germanici, praestitit genere ipso, probabilis in omnibus, sed in quibusdam suis ipse viribus minor.* "Servilius too was heard by us, a man of splendid talent and rich in apothegms, but with a style too rambling for the majesty of history. Aufidius Bassus, who was a little older, displayed that majesty splendidly in his manner of writing, particularly in the books dealing with the German War; he was admirable in all things, but sometimes fell short of his own powerful level." In Tacitus's *Dialogue* 23,2, Aper speaks of the *eloquentia* of both.

In addition to his treatment of the war against the Germans, Aufidius wrote a history whose starting point was during the period of the second triumvirate, perhaps soon after its establishment, and which continued to a point probably just prior to the death of Sejanus, from about 40 B.C. to about A.D. 30, although the close may be considerably later than that. More is known about Servilius, because Tacitus speaks of him further in the *Annals* (XIV:19) upon the occasion of his death: he had reached high office and been renowned for his oratorical ability, the elegance of his way of life, and his skill as a historian, *tradendis rebus Romanis*. Servilius was consul in A.D. 35, a year which still saw the effects of the reign of terror following upon the elimination of Sejanus, with Tiberius approaching the end of life. Servilius wrote the history of his own times, and his comments upon this period must have been rewarding indeed; it is a pity that the section of Tacitus's history dealing with these years has now been lost. Servilius must have particularly appealed to Tacitus because, like Tacitus himself, he was an example of the senator as historian. He wrote with an insight and understanding of public life that those who were not involved in the workings of the senatorial order could not have mastered.

Cluvius Rufus, another man involved in public life, is cited (*Hist.* IV:43,1) as being *dives et eloquentia clarus*, "wealthy and renowned for his eloquence." He is one of the prime sources for the later period covered in the *Annals* and indeed plays a role in it himself. He was one of the governors involved in the uprising against Nero, although his part was small, nay passive; not a man gifted in matters of war, his talents were those of the civilian (*Hist.* 1:8,1). Cluvius wrote the history of his own day, in all likelihood covering the reigns of Caligula, Claudius, and Nero. Pliny the Younger records a mild altercation that Cluvius had with Verginius Rufus (IX:19,5). Cluvius hoped that Verginius would not be offended by matter in his history that the latter would not like. The great man replied that he had acted as he had so that Cluvius might write what he wished. To what this conversation refers we can only conjecture.

Fabius Rusticus is cited by Tacitus three times, but his testimony must be used with caution; he was a close friend of Seneca (*cuius amicitia floruit, Ann.* XIII:20,2), and his portrait of that minister is therefore terribly biased. Consequently, his authority for Nero's reign is somewhat suspect; yet his prestige was great and his style justly renowned. Pliny the Elder covered much the same period as Cluvius Rufus, and he also wrote the history of the German wars. In the *Annals* Tacitus cites Pliny as the *Germanicorum bellorum scriptor* (1:69,2) and speaks of Pliny and Cluvius together as sources (XIII:20,2). Pliny, indeed, served Tacitus as a source for the *Germany* as well as for the *Histories* through personal experience of an extremely wide nature. Vipstanus Messalla, an important figure in the civil war, a junior officer who played a role far greater than his position might have suggested, was one whom Tacitus deeply admired (*Hist.* III:9,3). He is linked with Pliny as a source in the *Histories* (III:28). His memoirs must have been most useful.

With this survey one exhausts the roster of those major historians of the first century A.D. whom Tacitus was able to read and whom he felt compelled on occasion to correct. Their viewpoint of history is in part known. Fabius's bias for Seneca, with its corresponding bias against Nero, is an important factor in evaluating his work. Pliny, a tremendous polymath and scrupulous in research, was a strong supporter of the Flavian household, and his testimony is somewhat suspect on that score. But, nonetheless, these men were recognized historians, and it was they whom Tacitus was challenging when he undertook to write.

There were other sources. We know full well from Tacitus's own remarks that he was heavily involved in research. He sought out material which others, perhaps, had ignored or of which they were unaware. He cites the *Memoirs* of the younger Agrippina and of Corbulo. Since these of course were private records, the tendency is to oppose the accepted view of imperial history. Agrippina defends her mother against Tiberius and Corbulo gives his version of many of the events of the principates of Claudius and Nero.

For the *Agricola*, Tacitus was able to draw upon the experiences and conversation of his father-in-law. This is, of course, the first and most important source for any contemporary work, the recollections of the protagonist in the action, and thereby Tacitus was able to furnish information which no previous author had had available to him. His treatment of the *Germany* is different because there the material that he presents is very largely common knowledge, and indeed some of it, as the discussion of the *agri decumates* (29), is out-dated, for it does not fit the actual state of the German *limes* after Domitian's settlement. In this context he will have drawn upon the general fund of information gathered from the experience of travellers, merchants, and soldiers, and the works of authors like Pliny. But it is extremely unlikely that he was able to draw upon any personal experience, although one will have to recall that the man who may have been his father, as indicated in the first chapter, was a procurator in Germany. If this assumption is correct, then Tacitus may well have been able to draw upon information as personal as that of Agricola's in some parts of his work on Germany.

Further, he was able to consult the *acta senatus*, the records of the Senate, an extraordinarily important source of information accessible only to senators, and the public *acta diurna*, which were a chronicle of events of the city and empire. Geographers such as Pomponius Mela were available to him, and in some cases, as in the description of Britain, he is able to correct them. Pliny the Younger's letters about the eruption of Vesuvius were in response to inquiries from Tacitus for information to be laid under obligation for the *Histories*.

Nor should one ignore the circle of Tacitus's friends. As a member of the ruling aristocracy, he surely was able to inquire of events of men who had witnessed them or, like Verginius Rufus and Vipstanus Messalla, had been no little part of them. The extent of this unrecorded historical material is impossible to determine, but it must have been significant.

There are unknown historians whose existence we can discern only because of divergences in the accepted tradition among surviving writers. Tacitus's portrait of Tiberius is his most vivid. Details surely are his, yet the outline of Tiberius's life and the stages through which it was thought that he passed must have been firmly settled soon after the emperor's death. The historian responsible for this viewpoint is unknown to us. Yet we know from the treatments of Tacitus, Suetonius, and Dio Cassius that there were some elements upon which the three did not agree. Perhaps the most important is that which is known in German as the *Wendepunkt*, the turning point, of Tiberius's reign, the point at which he changed from a good to a bad emperor. Suetonius and Dio consider it to be caused by the death of Germanicus in 19, while Tacitus looks upon the death of Drusus, along with Sejanus's rise in 23, as the key.

In similar fashion the treatment of Galba, Otho, and, in part, Vitellius must have gone back to an accepted account written soon after the year of the four emperors. The divergences among Tacitus, Suetonius, and Plutarch in their handling of this material are revealing.

Tacitus's judgments on his predecessors, by no means always complimentary, are twice pronounced in broad terms in his major works. At the end of the second book of the *Histories* (101), he speaks disparagingly of the tradition of history under the Flavians which perverted events to flatter the Flavian dynasty and to indicate that their concern for the well-being of the commonwealth had been the only reason for Vespasian's rise: *Scriptores temporum, qui potiente rerum Flavia domo monimenta belli huiusce composuerunt, curam pacis et amorem rei publicae, corruptas in adulationem causas, tradidere: nobis super insitam levitatem et prodito Galba vilem mox fidem aemulatione etiam invidiaque, ne ab aliis apud Vitellium anteirentur, pervertisse ipsum Vitellium vi-*

dentur. "The historians of the period, who during the ascendancy of the Flavian family composed the chronicles of this war, have in the distorted representations of flattery assigned as the motives of these men a regard for peace and a love of their country. For my own part I believe that, to say nothing of a natural fickleness and an honour which they must have held cheap after the betrayal of Galba, feelings of rivalry, and jealousy lest others should outstrip them in the favour of Vitellius, made them accomplish his ruin." Tacitus clearly looked with a critical eye upon the histories of those years composed by men such as the elder Pliny.

In the last chapter of *Annals* II, when Tacitus commemorates Arminius's death with a splendid though brief obituary, he criticizes the lack of concern displayed by most writers for matters such as these: *liberator haud dubie Germaniae et qui non primordia populi Romani, sicut alii reges ducesque, sed florentissimum imperium lacessierit, proeliis ambiguus, bello non victus. septem et triginta annos vitae, duodecim potentiae explevit, caniturque adhuc barbaras apud gentes, Graecorum annalibus ignotus, qui sua tantum mirantur, Romanis haud perinde celebris, dum vetera extollimus recentium incuriosi.* "Assuredly he was the deliverer of Germany, one too who had defied Rome, not in her early rise, as other kings and generals, but in the height of her empire's glory, had fought, indeed, indecisive battles, yet in war remained unconquered. He completed thirty-seven years of life, twelve years of power, and he is still a theme of song among barbarous nations, though to Greek historians, who admire only their own achievements, he is unknown, and to Romans not as famous as he should be, while we extol the past and are indifferent to our own times." Tacitus evidently alludes to Livy's history here, and thereby raises Arminius to a position which will rival that of the greatest heroes of Livy's narrative. Yet, although his Roman predecessors are justly rebuked for their lack of concern with the contemporary events, the Greeks are bitterly attacked for their parochial interest only in their history. The intellectual climate of the second century A.D. in the Roman Empire featured a number of virtuoso Greeks whose achievements in oratory and diplomacy gave the age the prestige of the "Second Sophistic," but to Tacitus the Greeks of his day and the generations preceding had nothing to offer.

When one contemplates the sources of Tacitus's works, it is important to keep in mind that he was not writing history that did no more than reproduce the researches of his predecessors. For long modern scholarship believed that Tacitus's historical method was to use one major source. This source changed as the period treated changed, but that one source was put under obligation basically without alteration. In other words Tacitus was no more than a transcriber.

In more recent years scholars have shown that this was by no means the case. Tacitus was dependent upon the writers of previous history, as all historians who write of events that have attracted the attention of others have been and are, but he chose judiciously among his sources, totally dependent upon none, and very often, at crucial points, ignored the consensus of his predecessors to impose his own viewpoint and his own judgment. It is this historical insight and his skill in handling his sources that give Tacitus's history the freshness and the vigor that mark it. Not only the brilliance of style but the narrative power and the command of source material make his works exciting to read and intriguing to ponder.

VI. LANGUAGE AND STYLE

Tacitus's language and style follow in the tradition of Cato and Sallust. Very little of Cato has survived, but it is clear that he was Sallust's precedent; Sallust's work, on the other hand, has been preserved to a larger degree. Quintilian spoke admiringly of Sallust's *immortalis velocitas*, his "immortal swiftness," and it is perhaps this quality above all else that one discerns in Tacitus. Sallust's writing is likewise marked by *brevitas*, and in this he is not surpassed by Tacitus, who often has, contrary to general notions, quite long and involved sentences, with appendages to the main body of the sentence long after its end has been anticipated. What Tacitus does offer to a quite remarkable degree is the quality that Pliny mentioned and of which we have spoken earlier, σεμνότης, "majesty," which in Latin might be rendered *maiestas*, a dignity of style and language which raises the whole above the commonplace. Elevation is a characteristic of Tacitus's work both in theme and in vocabulary. He is interested neither in the colloquial nor in the routine, and often uses periphrases to avoid mentioning them. All in all, his is grand history and grand style.

Yet Tacitus was, one might almost say, an anachronism in his age, and a forerunner of what was to come. Quintilian, who held the first paid chair of Latin rhetoric at Rome by appointment of Vespasian, preached a clarity of style which was best exemplified by the language of Cicero. In this Quintilian went against the trend of his own age, in which Seneca, as Tacitus himself remarks, was able to please the great majority and to sum up, in his own rhetorical and seemingly artificial style, the taste of the day. Yet this flowery style was unappealing to Tacitus and, although no one could have forecast it, it was to become out of place under the emperor Hadrian. At that time archaism and preference for the ancient flourished, with Cato, for example, more popular than Livy. In such an intellectual climate, Seneca's virtuosity passed from favor.

Tacitus's style, however, was not the same throughout his life. It changed and developed, and this can be discerned not only from work to work, but within works, from one part to another, particularly in the last and fullest, the *Annals*. A number of features of his style deserve mention. There is the deliberate choice of words which have an archaic flavor, thereby confounding the general expectation of the reader of that day. There is a poetic quality, both in the choice of vocabulary and in construction, which calls to mind the favorite devices of Vergil and Lucan. Where synonyms exist, Tacitus tends invariably, as he becomes more mature, to prefer the less common, so that by the time of the *Annals* many words have disappeared from his vocabulary and have been supplanted by others. All these elements have shock value. They are essential for a brilliant and cutting style in which there are many phrases and sentences which can be plucked from context. His *sententiae* often have more than immediate validity and in their judgments become universal in application to the human condition. It is this quality that Aper seeks in the *Dialogue:* one must be able to carry specific thoughts home after hearing a speech, and it is these *sententiae* that he has in mind.

The style further is a "pointed" one. By "pointed" is meant a certain tension brought about not only by choice of words but by their position in contrast or in supplement so that a powerful effect follows and strikes upon the reader's senses as with a sledgehammer. As mentioned earlier, Tacitus's sentences are often quite long. He frequently delights in attaching ablatives, particularly absolutes, at the end of what seems to be the full thought, so that the sentence reels onward with subordinate construction depending upon subordinate construction long after one originally thought that the whole would come to an end. These additions often have great psychological power since they furnish a kind of inevitability to what is to come. Again, he often speaks in different places and in different tones about events still in the offing. In the earlier instances he is frequently very unclear about what will happen, yet the intimation as one reads is that what did occur was the only possible occurrence. As one looks back, one sees that the ultimate outcome was indeed forecast.

It is among some scholars an enterprise of considerable labor to break down Tacitus's language, style, and subject matter into separate entities, discerning how one affects the other. Yet one could reasonably say that the style is the man, and the subject matter and the language are all part of it. Certain subjects demand a certain style, and certain styles will best deal with a particular subject matter. There is a unity among the three elements that, in Tacitus, cannot be broken down, for without one the others will not exist.

Tacitus wrote in an age when the bulk of his output was quite remarkable. His chief rival in literature, as far as we can tell from what survives, was Pliny, whose hero was Cicero. Pliny tried to match his idol both in letters and in rhetoric and, although one will hardly say that he succeeded, nonetheless the effort deserves praise. Tacitus rivaled predecessors equally as early but no longer as popular, and herein is his great innovation, the fact that he made powerful and effective a style and method of treatment of history which had not, it seems, been used for several generations.

Tacitus has often been complimented for his psychology. He is, perhaps above all others, the virtuoso in the handling of the psychology of characters and of mood of narrative. His subject is, on the whole, a somber one, perhaps described for the entire corpus of his work by the beginning of the *Histories* as a difficult work full of bloodshed and war. Yet even beyond that he is in his narrative able to mold the mood of his readers by his subtle choice of potent words. Such is *arcanus*, referring to secrets and above all the secrets of what went on in the imperial household and the functioning of the principate, exemplified early in the *Histories* (1:4), when the secret of empire was revealed, that an emperor could be made elsewhere than in Rome. Another example is in the *Annals* (1:6), when Sallustius Crispus urges Livia not to permit the *arcana*, the secrets of rule, to be shared with the Senate. The word is the same; the impact is far greater; there has been a progression. In the *Histories*, an emperor can be made anywhere. This was obvious after the year which saw four emperors in succession. In the *Annals* we are no longer concerned with the making of an emperor, but rather with the unseen workings of his private establishment. So too with *dominatio*. It is a naughty and terrible word because a *dominus* at Rome is the equivalent of a *rex* elsewhere, not to be tolerated by free men. Tacitus uses ever increasingly the words *dominatio* and *dominus* in preference to *principatus* and *princeps* as the development of his historical work proceeds. In *Annals* 1:3, so early in the work, he comments that there were certain supports for Augustus's *dominatio*, and even though Tacitus had already mentioned that Augustus governed the empire with the title of *princeps*, here he boldly shows that *princeps* did not tell all. *Capax* is a word that Tacitus uses infrequently, but its implications are strong throughout. In the *Histories*, perhaps the most famous epitaph of all is that given Galba: *omnium consensu capax imperii, nisi imperasset* (1:49), "by common consent (he) would have been pronounced equal to empire, had he never been emperor." This seems to be one of Tacitus's large themes. Who were the men in the history of the early principate who were *capaces imperii?* Who would have served well had the opportunity arisen for them, as it did in the years 68–69 for Vespasian, a man certainly *capax* but destined to remain a private citizen under the tradition of choosing the emperor from the Julio-Claudian house? We shall return to this subject in chapter seven.

There are many other words that could be cited. Their repetition and subtle use undergird the entire corpus of Tacitus's work, with the result that they are potent factors in particular passages but also part of the psychological and philosophical development of the historian over a period of some twenty years.

Let us look at four passages from Tacitus's work to show how he made use of material and motifs that were at hand,

and yet was able to transcend them. The first that I wish to discuss is from the *Agricola*, the description of the scene of desolation and Caledonian despair after their defeat at Mons Graupius; its antecedent is in Sallust's *Jugurtha*, the aftermath of Marius's victory over the Numidians.

> *Et nox quidem gaudio praedaque laeta victoribus: Britanni palantes mixto virorum mulierumque ploratu trahere vulneratos, vocare integros, deserere domos ac per iram ultro incendere, eligere latebras et statim relinquere; miscere in vicem consilia aliqua, dein separare; aliquando frangi aspectu pignorum suorum, saepius concitari. satisque constabat saevisse quosdam in coniuges ac liberos, tamquam miserirentur. proximus dies faciem victoriae latius aperuit: vastum ubique silentium, secreti colles, fumantia procul tecta, nemo exploratoribus obvius.* (*Agricola* 38, 1–2)

And indeed night brought pleasure to the conquerors with rejoicing and booty: the Britons, scattering, with the mingled wailing of men and women, dragged their wounded along, called the uninjured, deserted their homes and with their own hands set them afire in anger, chose hiding places and immediately left them; they made some plans in common, then took them individually; sometimes they were crushed by the sight of their loved ones, more often driven to fury. And there was clear evidence that some laid violent hands on their wives and children as if they pitied them. The next day revealed more widely the appearance of victory: everywhere was overwhelming silence, desolate hills, houses smoking in the distance, no one found by the scouts.

> *tum spectaculum horribile in campis patentibus: sequi fugere, occidi capi; equi atque viri adflicti, ac multi volneribus acceptis neque fugere posse neque quietem pati, niti modo ac statim concidere; postremo omnia, qua visus erat, constrata telis armis cadaveribus, et inter ea humus infecta sanguine.* (*Jugurtha* 101, 11)

The broad plain presented a ghastly spectacle of flight and pursuit, slaughter and capture. Horses and men were thrown down; many of the wounded, without the strength to escape or the patience to lie still, struggled to get up, only to collapse immediately; as far as the eye could reach, the battlefield was strewn with weapons, armour, and corpses, with patches of bloodstained earth showing between them.

The very relation of these two narratives suggests an equation of Marius and Agricola. The latter's military prowess is clear enough, but to rank him with a Marius is extraordinary praise indeed. One notes, first of all, the extraordinary accumulation of historical infinitives, a device popular particularly among historians for its sensation of speed and rapidity. They number seven in Sallust, ten in Tacitus. Both authors make use of asyndeton, the lack of connectives. Sallust is here more vivid than Tacitus because his infinitives stand nakedly alone, whereas Tacitus has objects for each one and thereby slows the pace. Sallust's *spectaculum horribile in campis patentibus* is expanded and made more vivid by Tacitus's *proximus dies faciem victoriae latius aperuit: vastum ubique silentium.* The very word *faciem*, the human element of victory, gives an immediacy to Tacitus's statement that Sallust's lacks. Tacitus goes further still. He speaks of the emotions of the conquerors. In the first sentence *nox gaudio praedaque laeta victoribus* is immediately balanced by the terrible despair of the conquered, and is underscored by the equivalence of two unequivalent things: *gaudium*, a human emotion, and *praeda*, which is tangible, the result of conquest in war.

The next pair of passages presents the character sketches of Catiline and Sejanus, in the *Catiline* and the *Annals*. Once again, the reader who was familiar with Sallust's work and knew Catiline, his character, his deeds, and his end will have forecast comparable deeds and end for Sejanus from the similarity of their characters.

> *C. Asinio C. Antistio consulibus nonus Tiberio annus erat compositae rei publicae, florentis domus (nam Germanici mortem inter prospera ducebat), cum repente turbare fortuna coepit, saevire ipse aut saevientibus vires praebere. initium et causa penes Aelium Seianum, cohortibus praetoriis praefectum, cuius de potentia supra memoravi: nunc originem mores et quo facinore dominationem raptum ierit, expediam. genitus Vulsiniis patre Seio Strabone equite Romano, et prima iuventa C. Caesarem, divi Augusti nepotem, sectatus, non sine rumore Apicio diviti et prodigo stuprum veno dedisse, mox Tiberium variis artibus devinxit, adeo ut obscurum adversum alios sibi uni incautum intectumque efficeret, non tam sollertia (quippe isdem artibus victus est)*

quam deum ira in rem Romanam, cuius pari exitio viguit
ceciditque. corpus illi laborum tolerans, animus audax; sui
obtegens, in alios criminator; iuxta adulatio et superbia;
palam compositus pudor, intus summa apiscendi libido,
eiusque causa modo largitio et luxus, saepius industria ac
vigilantia, haud minus noxiae, quotiens parando regno fin-
guntur. (Annals IV: 1)

The year when Caius Asinius and Caius Antistius were
consuls was the ninth of Tiberius's reign, a period of tranquillity for the State and prosperity for his own house, for he
counted Germanicus's death a happy incident. Suddenly fortune deranged everything; the emperor became a cruel tyrant, as well as an abettor of cruelty in others. Of this the
cause and origin was Aelius Sejanus, commander of the praetorian cohorts, of whose influence I have already spoken. I
will now fully describe his extraction, his character, and the
daring wickedness by which he grasped at power.

Born at Vulsinii, the son of Seius Strabo, a Roman knight,
he attached himself in his early youth to Caius Caesar, grandson of the Divine Augustus, and the story went that he had
sold his person to Apicius, a rich debauchee. Soon afterwards
he won the heart of Tiberius so effectually by various artifices
that the emperor, ever dark and mysterious towards others,
was with Sejanus alone careless and freespoken. It was not
through his craft, for it was by this very weapon that he was
overthrown; it was rather from heaven's wrath against
Rome, to whose welfare his elevation and his fall were alike
disastrous. He had a body which could endure hardships, and
a daring spirit. He was one who screened himself, while he
was attacking others; he was as cringing as he was imperious;
before the world he affected humility; in his heart he lusted
after supremacy, for the sake of which he was sometimes
lavish and luxurious, but oftener energetic and watchful,
qualities quite as mischievous when hypocritically assumed
for the attainment of sovereignty.

L. Catilina, nobili genere natus, fuit magna vi et animi et
corporis, sed ingenio malo pravoque. huic ab adulescentia
bella intestina caedes rapinae discordia civilis grata fuere,
ibique iuventutem suam exercuit. corpus patiens inediae al-
goris vigiliae, supra quam quoiquam credibile est. animus
audax subdolus varius, quoius rei lubet simulator ac dissi-
mulator, alieni adpetens, sui profusus, ardens in cupiditati-

bus; satis eloquentiae, sapientiae parum. vastus animus inmo-
derata incredibilia nimis alta semper cupibat, hunc post
dominationem L. Sullae lubido maxuma invaserat rei pub-
licae capiundae; neque id quibus modis adsequeretur, dum
sibi regnum pararet, quicquam pensi habebat. agitabatur
magis magisque in dies animus ferox inopia rei familiaris
et conscientia scelerum, quae utraque iis artibus auxerat,
quas supra memoravi. incitabant praeterea conrupti civitatis
mores, quos pessuma ac divorsa inter se mala, luxuria atque
avaritia, vexabant. (Catiline 5, 1–8)

Lucius Catiline was of noble birth. He had a powerful in-
tellect and great physical strength, but a vicious and de-
praved nature. From his youth he had delighted in civil war,
bloodshed, robbery, and political strife, and it was in such
occupations that he spent his early manhood. He could endure hunger, cold, and want of sleep to an incredible extent.
His mind was daring, crafty, and versatile, capable of any
pretence and dissimulation. A man of flaming passions, he
was as covetous of other men's possessions as he was prodigal
of his own; an eloquent speaker, but lacking in wisdom. His
monstrous ambition hankered continually after things ex-
travagant, impossible, beyond his reach. After the dictatorship of Lucius Sulla, Catiline had been possessed by an over-
mastering desire for despotic power, to gratify which he was
prepared to use any and every means. His headstrong spirit
was tormented more and more every day by poverty and a
guilty conscience, both of which were aggravated by the evil
practices I have referred to. He was incited also by the corruption of a society plagued by two opposite but equally disastrous vices—love of luxury and love of money.

Sallust speaks of Catiline as *nobili genere natus*, Tacitus of
Sejanus as *patre equite Romano*. Catiline was a man of noble
rank, even a patrician, although that is not here mentioned;
Sejanus, on the contrary, is the son of a Roman knight, not
one of the aristocracy of Rome, and indeed later on Tacitus
will infuriatingly dub him a *municipalis* (a man from a mu-
nicipality). This will perhaps call to mind Catiline's similar
blast at Cicero as an *inquilinus Romanus*. Both men displayed
bad characters in their youth, *iuventutem* in one place, *iuventa*
in the other. Both are alike in their physical prowess, *corpus*

patiens matching *corpus tolerans*. Both have bold and daring minds; the precise words *animus audax* are in both authors, but Tacitus is more selective and penetrating. He simplifies his description and omits much with which Sallust had burdened his narrative but which he himself finds unnecessary. The effect of Tacitus's passage is more chaste. The ends, however, show a fundamental difference. Catiline wanted to gain the personal standing in the state of which he felt cheated, *lubido maxuma rei publicae capiundae; rei publicae capiundae* is an expression that need not be totally bad, for it is related to the perfectly respectable expression, *rem publicam capessere*, which refers to the active administration of public affairs. But his purpose was to gain personal dominance for himself, *dum sibi regnum pararet;* this too was Sejanus's aim, *parando regno,* yet the foreboding of doom is greater in Tacitus's narrative than in Sallust's, for the position of the words in the final clause in conjunction with the pejorative *finguntur* furnishes greater emphasis.

In *Annals* 1:9 and 10, Tacitus presents the varying comment of the people of Rome after the death of Augustus.

> *Multus hinc ipso de Augusto sermo, plerisque vana mirantibus: quod idem dies accepti quondam imperii princeps et vitae supremus, quod Nolae in domo et cubiculo, in quo pater eius Octavius, vitam finivisset. numerus etiam consulatuum celebrabatur, quo Valerium Corvum et C. Marium simul aequaverat, continuata per septem et triginta annos tribunicia potestas, nomen imperatoris semel atque vicies partum aliaque honorum multiplicata aut nova. at apud prudentes vita eius varie extollebatur arguebaturve. hi pietate erga parentem et necessitudine rei publicae, in qua nullus tunc legibus locus, ad arma civilia actum, quae neque parari possent neque haberi per bonas artes. multa Antonio, dum interfectores patris ulcisceretur, multa Lepido concessisse. postquam hic socordia senuerit, ille per libidines pessum datus sit, non aliud discordantis patriae remedium fuisse quam ut ab uno regeretur. non regno tamen neque dictatura, sed principis nomine constitutam rem publicam; mari Oceano aut amnibus longinquis saeptum imperium; legiones provincias classes, cuncta inter se conexa; ius apud cives, modestiam apud socios; urbem ipsam magnifico ornatu; pauca admodum vi tractata, quo ceteris quies esset.*

Dicebatur contra: pietatem erga parentem et tempora
rei publicae obtentui sumpta; ceterum cupidine dominandi
concitos per largitionem veteranos, paratum ab adulescente
privato exercitum, corruptas consulis legiones, simulatam
Pompeianarum gratiam partium. mox ubi decreto patrum
fasces et ius praetoris invaserit, caesis Hirtio et Pansa, sive
hostis illos, seu Pansam venenum vulneri adfusum, sui mi-
lites Hirtium et machinator doli Caesar abstulerat, utriusque
copias occupavisse; extortum invito senatu consulatum, ar-
maque quae in Antonium acceperit contra rem publicam
versa; proscriptionem civium, divisiones agrorum ne ipsis
quidem qui fecere laudatas. sane Cassii et Brutorum exitus
paternis inimicitiis datos, quamquam fas sit privata odia pub-
licis utilitatibus remittere: sed Pompeium imagine pacis, sed
Lepidum specie amicitiae deceptos; post Antonium, Taren-
tino Brundisinoque foedere et nuptiis sororis inlectum, sub-
dolae adfinitatis poenas morte exsolvisse. pacem sine dubio
post haec, verum cruentam: Lollianas Varianasque clades, in-
terfectos Romae Varrones Egnatios Iullos. nec domesticis ab-
stinebatur: abducta Neroni uxor et consulti per ludibrium
pontifices, an concepto necdum edito partu rite nuberet; Q.
Tedii (?) et Vedii Pollionis luxus; postremo Livia gravis in
rem publicam mater, gravis domui Caesarum noverca. nihil
deorum honoribus relictum, cum se templis et effigie nu-
minum per flamines et sacerdotes coli vellet. ne Tiberium qui-
dem caritate aut rei publicae cura successorem adscitum, sed,
quoniam adrogantiam saevitiamque eius introspexerit, com-
paratione deterrima sibi gloriam quaesivisse. etenim Augus-
tus paucis ante annis, cum Tiberio tribuniciam potestatem a
patribus rursum postularet, quamquam honora oratione,
quaedam de habitu cultuque et institutis eius iecerat, quae
velut excusando exprobraret. ceterum sepultura more per-
fecta templum et caelestes religiones decernuntur.

Then followed much talk about Augustus himself, and
many expressed an idle wonder that the same day marked
the beginning of his assumption of empire and the close of
his life, and, again, that he had ended his days at Nola in the
same house and room as his father Octavius. People extolled
too the number of his consulships, in which he had equalled
Valerius Corvus and Caius Marius combined, the contin-
uance for thirty-seven years of the tribunitian power, the title
of Imperator twenty-one times earned, and his other honours
which had been either frequently repeated or were wholly

new. Sensible men, however, spoke variously of his life with praise and censure. Some said "that dutiful feeling towards a father, and the necessities of the State in which laws had then no place, drove him into civil war, which can neither be planned nor conducted on any right principles. He had often yielded to Antonius, while he was taking vengeance on his father's murderers, often also to Lepidus. When the latter sank into feeble dotage and the former had been ruined by his profligacy, the only remedy for his distracted country was the rule of a single man. Yet the State had been organized under the name neither of a kingdom nor a dictatorship, but under that of a prince. The ocean and remote rivers were the boundaries of the empire; the legions, provinces, fleets, all things were linked together; there was law for the citizens; there was respect shown to the allies. The capital had been embellished on a grand scale; only in a few instances had he resorted to force, simply to secure general tranquillity."

It was said, on the other hand, "that filial duty and State necessity were merely assumed as a mask. It was really from a lust of sovereignty that he had excited the veterans by bribery, had, when a young man and a subject, raised an army, tampered with the Consul's legions, and feigned an attachment to the faction of Pompeius. Then, when by a decree of the Senate he had usurped the high functions and authority of Praetor, when Hirtius and Pansa were slain— whether they were destroyed by the enemy, or Pansa by poison infused into a wound, Hirtius by his own soldiers and Caesar's treacherous machinations—he at once possessed himself of both their armies, wrested the consulate from a reluctant Senate, and turned against the State the arms with which he had been intrusted against Antonius. Citizens were proscribed, lands divided, without so much as the approval of those who executed these deeds. Even granting that the deaths of Cassius and of the Bruti were sacrifices to a hereditary enmity (though duty requires us to waive private feuds for the sake of the public welfare), still Pompeius had been deluded by the phantom of peace, and Lepidus by the mask of friendship. Subsequently, Antonius had been lured on by the treaties of Tarentum and Brundisium, and by his marriage with the sister, and paid by his death the penalty of a treacherous alliance. No doubt, there was peace after all this, but it was a peace stained with blood; there were the disasters of Lollius and Varus, the murders at Rome of the Varros, Egnatii, and Juli."

The domestic life too of Augustus was not spared. "Nero's wife had been taken from him, and there had been the farce of consulting the pontiffs, whether, with a child conceived and not yet born, she could properly marry. There were the excesses of Quintus Tedius and Vedius Pollio; last of all, there was Livia, terrible to the State as a mother, terrible to the house of the Caesars as a stepmother. No honour was left for the gods, when Augustus chose to be himself worshipped with temples and statues, like those of the deities, and with flamens and priests. He had not even adopted Tiberius as his successor out of affection or any regard to the State, but, having thoroughly seen his arrogant and savage temper, he had sought glory for himself by a contrast of extreme wickedness." For, in fact, Augustus, a few years before, when he was a second time asking from the Senate the tribunitian power for Tiberius, though his speech was complimentary, had thrown out certain hints as to his manners, style, and habits of life, which he meant as reproaches, while he seemed to excuse. However, when his obsequies had been duly performed, a temple with a religious ritual was decreed him.

Augustus had already received much attention from Tacitus. One need only recall the use of the word *dominatio* in chapter three to set the mood. In these two chapters, Tacitus's skill in placing and arranging his material is paramount; the last judgments will be the ones most easily remembered. Chapter nine is briefer than ten; its subject is the favorable. Yet it begins almost with an air of unreality because the first items are trivial and coincidental; they have no role to play in the man's career and posterity's judgment of it. The majority of people characteristically are concerned with the unimportant. Then there is a sudden shift to the *prudentes*, the more discerning people, the ones who know. The narrative immediately takes a different turn. It begins with the adversative *at*, and the emperor's life is praised or faulted, *extollebatur arguebaturve. Pietas erga parentem* and *necessitudo rei publicae*, the chief motives for his actions in forty-four, recall the first two chapters of Augustus's own testament, the *Res gestae*. Antony and Lepidus were just shunted aside; the reader will recall the extremely powerful verb used in connection with

Lepidus in chapter two, *exuto*, "cast off," just as one can remove a coat. Finally at the end, there is a grudging tribute indeed: *mari Oceano aut amnibus longinquis saeptum imperium; legiones provincias classes, cuncta inter se conexa; ius apud cives, modestiam apud socios; urbem ipsam magnifico ornatu; pauca admodum vi tractata, quo ceteris quies esset.* *Ius* and *modestia* will perhaps come to mind in the reading of III:28,1, where Tacitus emphasizes the absence of law and order in the late republic, *non mos, non ius.*

In chapter ten, *pietas* and *tempora rei publicae* immediately challenge the previous chapter. Augustus's critics, of course, look at these claims from quite a different point of view. *Dominandi* is once more an ominous word, and *privato*, again recalling the beginning of the *Res gestae*, underscores the illegality of his actions, most particularly his dependence upon a personal army. Then follows a section which reeks of innuendo, concerning the deaths of Hirtius and Pansa, whether the enemy killed them or Octavian was treacherously responsible for their ends; there is no evidence that there was any ill-doing, yet the suggestion is strong. The consulate was extorted from an unwilling Senate, *extortum* and *invito*. The word *sane* is supercilious. The clause *pacem sine dubio post haec, verum cruentam* will put the conclusion of the preceding chapter in a different light. There appeared the statement that the world was basically at peace; here is a list of disasters and a recitation of people killed, all of them in the plural, "Men like so and so," with the intimation that these were not unusual and spare occurrences, but common and continuous. Augustus's personal failings are outlined. Livia is described as a heavy burden to the household and the commonwealth. *Nihil deorum honoribus relictum* contradicts Augustus's own feelings about the imperial cult, for in Italy and the provinces of the West he was quite chary in permitting worship of himself. And finally there is a slap at both Augustus and Tiberius, along with the comment that Augustus had underscored Tiberius's personal failings in the very act of designating him his colleague. Nothing in this chapter may indeed be untrue, yet little can be said to be certainly true. Tacitus's handling of the material is such that the reader is left with a very bad taste in his mouth.

The next comparison will be between Claudius's speech on the admission of the Gallic chieftains to the Senate, preserved in part on a bronze tablet that was found at Lyons in the year 1528, and Tacitus's version of it in *Annals* XI:24. This is the only instance in ancient history where scholars have an opportunity to compare an ancient speech with a literary version of it. It is extremely revealing, and one surely would hope, for example, that Pericles's funeral oration might someday be found on a stone so that we could see what Thucydides did with that raw material. The Latin texts are omitted because of the length of Claudius's speech. The translation of the Tacitean passage follows first.

These and like arguments failed to impress the emperor. He at once addressed himself to answer them, and thus harangued the assembled Senate. "My ancestors, the most ancient of whom was made at once a citizen and a noble of Rome, encourage me to govern by the same policy of transferring to this city all conspicuous merit, wherever found. And indeed I know, as facts, that the Julii came from Alba, the Coruncanii from Camerium, the Porcii from Tusculum, and not to inquire too minutely into the past, that new members have been brought into the Senate from Etruria and Lucania and the whole of Italy, that Italy itself was at last extended to the Alps, to the end that not only single persons but entire countries and tribes might be united under our name. We had unshaken peace at home; we prospered in all our foreign relations, in the days when Italy beyond the Po was admitted to share our citizenship, and, when, enrolling in our ranks the most vigorous of the provincials, under colour of settling our legions throughout the world, we recruited our exhausted empire. Are we sorry that the Balbi came to us from Spain, and other men not less illustrious from Narbon Gaul? Their descendants are still among us, and do not yield to us in patriotism.

"What was the ruin of Sparta and Athens, but this, that mighty as they were in war, they spurned from them as aliens those whom they had conquered? Our founder Romulus, on the other hand, was so wise that he fought as enemies and then hailed as fellow-citizens several nations on the very same day. Strangers have reigned over us. That freedmen's sons should be intrusted with public offices is not, as many wrongly think, a sudden innovation, but was a common practice in the old commonwealth. But, it will be said, we have fought with the Senones. I suppose then that the Volsci and Aequi never stood in array against us. Our city was taken by the Gauls. Well, we also gave hostages to the Etruscans, and passed under the yoke of the Samnites. On the whole, if you review all our wars, never has one been finished in a shorter time than that with the Gauls. Thenceforth they have preserved an unbroken and loyal peace. United as they now are with us by manners, education, and intermarriage, let them bring us their gold and their wealth rather than enjoy it in isolation. Everything, Senators, which we now hold to be of the highest antiquity, was once new. Plebeian magistrates came after patrician; Latin magistrates after plebeian; magistrates of other Italian peoples after Latin. This practice too will establish itself, and what we are this day justifying by precedents, will be itself a precedent."

The manner of the Emperor's rhetoric is quite different, even in translation.

As a matter of fact, I deprecate that first impression which I foresee in the minds of all men that I shall encounter, as my first and greatest obstacle, and I beg of you not to be alarmed, as if some novelty were being proposed, but rather to consider these facts: how many innovations have been introduced in this city and indeed into how many different patterns and shapes our State has been fitted from the very beginning of our city.

Formerly this city was ruled by kings, who, however, did not transmit the sovereignty by hereditary succession. The succession went to other families and even to foreigners. So Romulus was succeeded by Numa, who came from the Sabines, a neighboring tribe, to be sure, but at that time a foreign people. So Tarquinius Priscus succeeded Ancus Marcius. The former was the son of the Corinthian Demaratus and a Tarquinian mother of noble blood, but impoverished, as she must have been to make such a marriage. Since he was barred from public office at home because of the taint in his blood, he migrated to Rome and obtained the kingship. Between him and his son or his grandson, for on this point the sources disagree, Servius Tullius interrupted the succession. According to Roman tradition, he was the son of Ocresia, a prisoner of war, but according to Etruscan sources he was once a most loyal comrade of Caelius Vivenna and shared in all his adventures. After he was expelled from Etruria by a shift in fortune, he took the remnants of Caelius' army and occupied the hill that took its name from that commander. Then, when he changed his name, for he was called Mastarna in Etruscan, he took the name that I have mentioned, and he held the kingship, to the greatest advantage of the State. Later, when the character of Tarquinius Superbus as well as of his sons grew odious to our State, the mind of the people became thoroughly sick of kingship and the government of the State was transferred to annual magistrates, the consuls.

To what purpose now should I remind you of the power of the dictatorship, greater even than that of the consuls, devised by our ancestors for use in the more dangerous wars or in the more critical civil disturbances? Or of the plebeian tribunes created for the protection of the plebs? Or of the transfer of power from the consuls to the decemvirs and, when their royal power was broken, of its return again to the consuls? Or of the consular power being shared yearly with several, even as many as six or eight, called military tribunes with consular power? Or of the privilege of holding magistracies and even priesthoods, finally shared with the plebeians? For if I were to tell the story of our wars from the beginning under our ancestors and how far we have advanced, I am afraid that I may seem somewhat vainglorious and to have sought an excuse for boasting of my own extension of the bounds of empire beyond the ocean. But let me return rather to the point. Citizenship. . . .

As a matter of fact, it was an innovation that both the deified Augustus, my great-uncle, and my uncle Tiberius Caesar wished to have in this House all the flower of the colonies and of the cities everywhere, that is, the men of worth and wealth. But, you object, is not an Italian preferable to a provincial as a senator? When I come to justify this part of my censorship to you, I shall show what I think about this by my acts. But I do not think that even provincials should be excluded, if they can be an ornament to this House.

Mark you! That most distinguished and most powerful colony of Vienne already for a long time has contributed senators to this House. From this colony comes Lucius Vestinus, one of the chief ornaments of our equestrian order, whom I cherish as a most intimate friend and whom I still employ in my service. I desire that his children shall enjoy the highest rank in priestly offices and that they in years to come shall be promoted to offices of increasing dignity. Let me pass over the ill-omened name of the bandit—and I despise that monster of the wrestling school—who won the consulship for his family before his colony had gained the full benefits of Roman citizenship. I can say the same of his brother, who could not be of service to you as a senator, on account of this wretched and most ignoble end.

Now, Tiberius Germanicus Caesar, it is time for you to reveal to the conscript fathers how far your speech is going, for you already have reached the farthest limits of Narbonnese Gaul!

Mark you! These many distinguished youths whom I see before me will give us no more cause for regret if admitted as senators than it does to my friend Persicus, a man of highest distinction, to read the name of Allobrogicus among the images of his ancestors. But if you admit that this is true, what further proof do you need than my pointing out that lands beyond the bounds of Narbonnese Gaul are already sending senators to you, when we do not regret to have members from Lyon?

It is with some hesitation, indeed, conscript fathers, that I have gone beyond the bounds of old and familiar provinces, but now I must plead briefly the cause of Gallia Comata. In this matter, if anyone looks to the fact that these people fought for ten years against the deified Julius, he may set against that 100 years of unwavering loyalty and an obedience which was tested to the utmost on many occasions, when our own fortunes were quite critical. When my father Drusus was subduing Germany, it was they who by their tranquillity provided undisturbed and profound peace in his rear—and that too, although he was called to war while taking the census, which was at that time a new and strange imposition for the Gauls. How difficult a task the census is for us, even in this present day, we have learned by bitter experience, although nothing is required from us beyond an official record of our resources.

Tacitus has often been charged with complete misrepresentation of Claudius's arguments, twisting his words to make him sound like a buffoon. This is hardly true. What Tacitus has done is to take the emperor's rambling speech, marked by pedantry and reference to self, make it fit into his own narrative in an appropriate style, and yet retain some of Claudius's qualities, particularly in the use of archaism. Tacitus has produced a shorter speech, a tighter speech, and one which therefore has greater impact. It is far more effective.

Claudius's speech is so long (the surviving portion represents only about half the original length) and proceeds so generally in a chronological manner that all emphasis and focus are destroyed. The impression a reader obtains is that the Roman State, from its beginning, has welcomed foreigners into its citizen body and its ruling class. The emperor points out that the state profited from this accession in the past, but fails to show what advantage his principate will obtain to the satisfaction of the members of the senatorial order, whose perquisites will of course be diluted by expansion of their number. Claudius was a historian who had been a pupil of Livy, and his tendency to digress with minutiae is nowhere more evident than in the rendition of details in the life of Tarquinius Priscus. But these details make a speech difficult to follow for an audience; that Claudius realized this is shown by the outburst from a senator (some editors consider this a self-allocution): "Now, Tiberius Germanicus Caesar, it is time for you to reveal to the conscript fathers how far your speech is going, for you already have reached the farthest limits of Narbonnese Gaul!"

Tacitus molds this raw material into a convincing exhortation with a double theme: the empire is suffering fatigue which will be healed by adding these vigorous Gauls to the senatorial rolls and there will be substantial profit because their wealth will be available for the service of the state. Nor does he follow a strictly chronological pattern; names are presented where they will have the greatest effect. Tacitus chooses to use the generalizing plural—*Iulios, Coruncanios, Porcios*—rather than accumulate a series of names. In time past, the worn-out empire prospered by a transfusion of new blood, *fesso imperio subventum est;* the same will surely occur in the present circumstances, for the situation is the same. Mention of Romulus, *conditor nostri*, gains in impact by being delayed; and his wisdom, superior to that of the greatest Greek states, is invoked. Even the sons of freedmen, *libertinorum filiis*, have held magistracies; may one discern here an example of Tacitus's impatience with the power of freedmen in Claudius's reign? Gaul has been long pacified, *continua ac fida pax*, and it is prosperous; Rome should wish to share this prosperity, *aurum et opes suas inferant potius quam separati habeant*. And Tacitus concludes with an appeal to the *mores maiorum*, the body of tradition that had accumulated over the centuries; the Senate should not fear novelty in the emperor's proposal, for everything was once an innovation, *omnia, quae nunc vetustissima creduntur, nova fuere*, and the present decision will become part of tradition, *inveterascet hoc quoque inter exempla erit*.

This chapter has underscored some of the characteristics of Tacitus's Latin and his handling of the language. To read Tacitus, particularly his late works, is a thrill that can be matched by perhaps no other author in the Latin language with the possible exception of Vergil. There is a power and a sweep and a loftiness which continue for hundreds of pages that are almost beyond compare. But style will not readily survive translation into another language. No matter how skillful a translation may be, an author's intangible qualities will be lost.

VII. CHARACTERIZATION: HEROES AND VILLAINS

The pace and tension of Tacitus's narratives are supported by his skill in characterization. Throughout his works a substantial number of important individuals is developed to a greater or lesser degree. There are not many whose influence spans a series of books, and who are developed as characters over that period of time. In spite of that some of his most notable presentations are those whom he delineates briefly and often only once. Tacitus's characters are not only individuals but often also represent types; thus one can see the type of the sage or the tyrant or the *delator*, the informer, as well as a precise person, in the presentation of certain people. Very often Tacitus outlines his judgment of an individual either when the person is first introduced or at his death. These are brief and penetrating; they either forecast the action that the person will be responsible for or recapitulate his life and often, through the life, part of the age. Obituaries are an important feature of Tacitus's treatment both of individuals and of his philosophy of history.

It will be fruitful to consider the works in their order to see how he handles the characters who march across the stage and to discern whether there is any development in his treatment of them. In the *Agricola* the only person whom we get to know well and in depth is the hero. The others are presented either as backdrops for his actions or as names to fill out the narrative. A few such as Petilius Cerialis and Sextus Julius Frontinus are complimented, though briefly, to such a degree that one realizes that they are men of quality. But there is no characterization, and they themselves do not appear. Agricola, however, as is appropriate for the subject of a biography, is carried from birth to death; and we see him not only in moments of glory but also with his frailties, so that we get a more balanced picture of him than of any other individual in Tacitus's work.

In the *Germany* there is no character development. The nature of the work is against it, and practically no individuals are mentioned. In the *Dialogue* the participants in the discussion are all outlined to a certain degree, but Aper is the one whom we get to know best. It is he whose violent enthusiasm is underscored most fully, and who is given a major role in the capacity, it may be, of devil's advocate. It is often said that Maternus represents Tacitus himself and, consequently, one will perhaps examine that figure more closely than any other. But the relationship deals not with character but with belief in the primacy of literary form over oratory.

In the *Histories* Vespasian and Mucianus are presented early and together (II:5). Yet it is Mucianus about whom more is said and upon whom attention is focused for a large part of the work. It is he who is responsible for persuading Vespasian to claim the purple (II:76–77); it is he who, on the march to Italy and then after arrival in Rome, is at the center of action while Vespasian is still off, hidden away, so to speak, in the East. Mucianus is a man who had many of the qualities which would have made a good emperor. But he did not have the highest, a scrupulous character which is content with the negation of self for the betterment of the state. Mucianus's characterization develops over a number of books. Indeed, had we the whole of the *Histories*, we might have a great deal more which would fill out even further the picture that we have of him.

The first three emperors of this fateful year are presented in full—Galba more sympathetically, in spite of the harsh words Tacitus occasionally uses, than his two immediate successors. Galba was an old man whose potential for rule had been forecast by Tiberius more than thirty years earlier (*Ann.* VI:20). He was an anachronism in his brief tenure of the principate, more concerned with the old virtues of the Roman people than the age could then tolerate. His attempt to rule was laudable, but his method of doing so was totally passé. He began badly at his first entry into Rome, with bloodshed, although this is not included in the narrative; and, at his first appearance in the *Histories*, the days and the events are ill-omened. The end is equally sombre, with his murder in the forum within sight of the Palatine, the temples on the Capitoline, and the senate house. In many respects Galba appears to be a literary characterization more than any other. There are parallels between his last day and the death of Priam in Vergil's *Aeneid*. It may well be that Tacitus, beyond drawing upon Vergil for vocabulary and construction, in this instance used some of Vergil's narrative for the end, a nonheroic and pathetic end, of a man who had been head of a great state. Both are old; both at the crucial moment don a breastplate, the incongruity of which, for their age and position, underscores their futility. Both, when murdered, are left as headless corpses, bodies lying neglected. Both are slain near a sacred place, Priam near an altar, Galba near the Lacus Curtius. This very conjunction of holy places with foul murder forecasts clearly that the events to follow cannot be good. Priam's death was a part of the destruction of his city, which was already underway. Galba's death was the first one of a sequence that almost culminated in the destruction of Rome in a year which was, as Tacitus said, well nigh the last of the existence of city and commonwealth. Galba's obituary (1:49) is justly famous, concluding with what is perhaps Tacitus's best-known epitaph.

> Such was the end of Servius Galba, who in his seventy-three years had lived prosperously through the reigns of five Emperors, and had been more fortunate under the rule of others than he was in his own. His family could boast an ancient nobility, his wealth was great. His character was of an average kind, rather free from vices, than distinguished by virtues. He was not regardless of fame, nor yet vainly fond of it. Other men's money he did not covet, with his own he was parsimonious, with that of the State avaricious. To his freed-

men and friends he shewed a forbearance, which, when he had fallen into worthy hands, could not be blamed; when, however, these persons were worthless, he was even culpably blind. The nobility of his birth and the perils of the times made what was really indolence pass for wisdom. While in the vigour of life, he enjoyed a high military reputation in Germany; as proconsul he ruled Africa with moderation, and when advanced in years shewed the same integrity in Eastern Spain. He seemed greater than a subject while he was yet in a subject's rank, and by common consent would have been pronounced equal to empire, had he never been emperor.

Otho begins badly. His accession to the throne is marked by murder and treachery, but his career as emperor, brief though it is, continues on a rising note. His behavior following a brief mutiny of troops that threatened his own life and the lives of many senators, when he expresses, in a speech that may be totally Tacitus's own (1:83–84), his belief in the importance of the Senate, speaks well for ideals gaining the upper hand over opportunism. His actions on the battlefield, although occasionally marked by confusion and doubt, at the end win him high praise. When defeated at the first battle of Bedriacum, he is unwilling to squander Roman blood further and willingly commits suicide in the fashion of the great *imperatores* of old. It may be that this can be considered a *devotio*, a dedication of his own person to gain a worthy end for the enterprise at hand. Otho's obituary (II:49–50) reveals Tacitus's judgment, but the reader has had an opportunity to see, in a span of a full book covering fewer than four months, how Otho's actions could justify Tacitus's statement.

Towards evening he quenched his thirst with a draught of cold water. Two daggers were brought to him; he tried the edge of each, and then put one under his head. After satisfying himself that his friends had set out, he passed a tranquil night, and it is even said that he slept. At dawn he fell with his breast upon the steel. Hearing a groan from the dying man, his freedmen and slaves, and Plotius Firmus, prefect of the Praetorian Guard, came in. They found but one wound. His funeral was hastily performed. He had made this the subject of earnest entreaties, anxious that his head might not be cut off and subjected to indignities. The Praetorian cohorts carried his body with praises and tears, covering his wound and his hands with kisses. Some of the soldiers killed themselves near the funeral pile, not moved by remorse or by fear, but by the desire to emulate his glory, and by love of their Prince. Afterwards this kind of death became a common practice among all ranks at Bedriacum, at Placentia, and in the other camps. Over Otho was built a tomb unpretending and therefore likely to stand.

Thus Otho ended his life in the 37th year of his age. He came from the municipal town of Ferentinum. His father was of consular, his grandfather of praetorian rank. His family on the mother's side was of less distinction, but yet respectable. What his boyhood and his youth had been, we have already shewn. By two daring acts, one most atrocious, the other singularly noble, he earned in the eyes of posterity about an equal share of infamy and of glory.

Vitellius begins equally badly, but unlike Otho he never improves. His reign is one of debauchery, inability, and cowardice. More than with Galba and with Otho, it is the lesser characters, particularly the generals Caecina and Valens, who hold center stage. From their first appearances, when they urge and support Vitellius's claim of the purple, they are personifications of evil and treachery. And the behavior of their armies on the march south into Italy supports every possible unfavorable conclusion about them.

Vitellius dies late in Book III, with an end worthy of an unworthy life, a man who had had no recommendation for rule other than the distinction of his father. During the Vitellius books, the prime figure is not a supporter of the reigning emperor but an unexpected ally of the new claimant, Vespasian. This is Antonius Primus who perhaps more than anyone else in the *Histories* comes closest to Sejanus. Tacitus's introduction of him (II:86) indicates an evil nature and bespeaks his speed of action.

This man, though an offender against the law, and convicted of fraud in the reign of Nero, had, among the other calamities of war, recovered his rank as a Senator. Having been appointed by Galba to command the 7th legion, he was commonly believed to have often written to Otho, offering the party his services as a general. Being slighted, however, by that Prince, he found no employment during the war. When the fortunes of Vitellius began to totter, he attached himself to Vespasian, and brought a vast accession of strength to his party. He was brave in battle, ready of speech, dexterous in bringing odium upon other men, powerful amidst civil strife and rebellion, rapacious, prodigal, the worst of citizens in peace, but in war no contemptible ally.

It is he who gains the imperium for Vespasian by his almost Caesarian maneuvers long before Vespasian could otherwise have hoped for success. Although unexpected, Antonius's support was crucial. But when Mucianus arrives in Italy, it is he who occupies the chief position and Primus is gradually shunted into the background.

Tacitus's chief achievement in the delineation of character, the emperor Tiberius, appears in the *Annals*. Tiberius's reign covers the first six books; and from the beginning, with remarks such as those in I:10, where Augustus lamented his unpleasant character when presenting him to the Senate as his colleague, to the end of Book VI, one has the picture of a gloomy, morose, bitter man who at the last becomes a tyrant. All this is perhaps true. How much was Tacitus's own judgment, how much stems from the standard picture of Tiberius's reign that developed soon after his death, we do not know. It is likely that Tacitus believed a great deal of it; he seldom, however, defends Tiberius although some opportunities existed. This will be discussed later in the chapter on historical integrity.

There are numerous places throughout the first six books where the character of Tiberius is underscored. Everything culminates in VI:51 where the stages of Tiberius's life are sketched and Tacitus goes back beyond the beginning of Tiberius's reign in A.D. 14 to trace his life from the very beginning. This is one of the very few instances in the narrative where Tacitus ignores his self-imposed starting date.

Although Tiberius is the classic figure, Germanicus, Agrippina, and Sejanus are worthy counterpoints. Germanicus occupies center stage for much of the first two books and his shade is still important for the first third of the next. Germanicus, it is often said, was Tacitus's hero, the one whom he would have liked to see reign in place of Tiberius. This may be true. Yet the picture that Tacitus paints of Germanicus is by no means uniformly favorable. His first appearance in Book I follows upon that of his adoptive brother Drusus after Drusus had successfully, and with honor, put down the revolt of the Pannonian legions. Germanicus himself is less effective in accomplishing the same in Germany, and it is only after grandstanding behavior and promises bordering on treason that he is able to recover the allegiance of his troops.

The importance of Agrippina, a woman of character almost stronger than a man's, is already evident in this context when her departure from the camp with the young Gaius is, above all, the act which brings the maddened soldiers to their senses. In general she seems to be much more hard-headed than Germanicus, who is presented as somewhat of a romantic. He delights in the unusual and the noteworthy. He is eager to visit the site of Varus's debacle in the Teutoburg Forest and to perform burial rites which his membership in a priestly college forbade him to do. Tiberius disapproved because of the debilitating effect this would have upon the army. When Germanicus has been recalled from Germany and is on his way to the East, he makes a grand tour, visiting the sights of antiquity, and enters Egypt, contrary to the precedent of Augustus to which Tiberius scrupulously adhered that no senator should do so without express permission; there he presents himself, so to speak, as a new Alexander, and thereby again courts Tiberius's disfavor. Nonetheless, he is a man of talent and, when he dies, Tacitus's judgment that he was comparable to Alexander and in some respects superior can be taken seriously. With him there is a progression upwards. He dies a hero, all his faults forgotten. It is remembered that he had a *civile ingenium*, "an affable nature," and that in the public mind he would have restored the republic had the rule become his. The military losses have disappeared from memory; the triumphs have remained. Agrippina now comes to the fore, her resentment and anger at her husband's death vividly presented, both during her return to Italy and as part of the court proceedings against Piso. She appears intermit-

tently in subsequent books as the focus of opposition to Tiberius and Sejanus until she and almost all the members of
her family are destroyed.

Sejanus has already been discussed in part above. His appearance in Book IV, though it comes like a clash of thunder,
has been forecast earlier in the work. He is not a new character,
but he is now introduced as far more powerful than one might
have anticipated before. His winning of Tiberius's confidence
and trust is shown gradually, culminating, perhaps, in the
scene at Spelunca when he protected the emperor from bodily
harm in the cave's collapse (IV:59). One of the chief losses
of the corpus of Tacitus's work is the part of Book V which
would have dealt with the destruction of this great minister.

When the narrative resumes after a gap of some ten years,
Gaius's entire reign and the first six years of Claudius, we are
in the midst of the reign of the man so often derided as a buffoon and the plaything of his wives and freedmen. They are
presented with broad strokes; Messalina and the younger
Agrippina, Pallas and Narcissus play the chief roles in the
surviving Claudian books. Agrippina survives into the reign
of her son and, indeed, is shown at the beginning of Book XIV,
in that remarkable section where her murder is described, to
have been a most astonishingly powerful, malelike figure,
domineering and tough. But she met her match in Poppaea
Sabina, who is introduced in one of Tacitus's most remarkable
characterizations (XIII:45). She was a woman blessed with
all advantages save honor, and was willing to subordinate
everything to her lust for power. Though married, she attracted first Otho and then the emperor himself; and when he
had to choose between her and his mother, he chose her.

> Non minus insignis eo anno impudicitia magnorum rei
> publicae malorum initium fecit. erat in civitate Sabina Pop-
> paea, T. Ollio patre genita, sed nomen avi materni sump-
> serat, inlustri memoria Poppaei Sabini consularis et trium-
> phali decore praefulgentis; nam Ollium honoribus nondum
> functum amicitia Seiani pervertit. huic mulieri cuncta alia
> fuere praeter honestum animum. quippe mater eius, aetatis
> suae feminas pulchritudine supergressa, gloriam pariter et
> formam dederat; opes claritudini generis sufficiebant. sermo
> comis nec absurdum ingenium. modestiam praeferre et las-

civia uti; rarus in publicum egressus, idque velata parte oris,
ne satiaret adspectum, vel quia sic decebat. famae numquam
pepercit, maritos et adulteros non distinguens; neque ad-
fectui suo aut alieno obnoxia, unde utilitas ostenderetur, illuc
libidinem transferebat.

A profligacy equally notorious in that same year proved
the beginning of great evils to the State. There was at Rome
one Sabina Poppaea; her father was Titus Ollius, but she had
assumed the name of her maternal grandfather Poppaeus Sabinus, a man of illustrious memory and pre-eminently distinguished by the honours of a consulship and a triumph. As
for Ollius, before he attained promotion, the friendship of
Sejanus was his ruin. This Poppaea had everything but a
right mind. Her mother, who surpassed in personal attractions all the ladies of her day, had bequeathed to her alike
fame and beauty. Her fortune adequately corresponded to
the nobility of her descent. Her conversation was charming
and her wit anything but dull. She professed virtue, while
she practised laxity. Seldom did she appear in public, and it
was always with her face partly veiled, either to disappoint
men's gaze or to set off her beauty. Her character she never
spared, making no distinction between a husband and a
paramour, while she was never a slave to her own passion or
to that of her lover. Wherever there was a prospect of advantage, there she transferred her favours.

When Nero becomes emperor, he promises in his speech
from the throne that there will be a return to the constitutional
rule of Augustus's principate. The words were Seneca's, yet
the very beginning of Book XIII, with the statement that the
first murder of the new reign was the death of Junius Silanus,
recalls the beginning of Tiberius's reign with the murder of
Agrippa Postumus; Tacitus forecasts very clearly that the fact
will be very different from the claim. Nero develops only
slightly. As he grows from young manhood to maturity and
becomes fully aware of the power that he wields as princeps,
the influence of others upon him correspondingly decreases.
Hence the roles of Seneca and Burrus gradually diminish;
Thrasea, the champion of the opposition, becomes more important. Burrus generally comes off well although his role is
not a major one; the picture presented is that of an honest
soldier, capable and loyal to his oath, with perhaps only par-

ticipation in the approval of Agrippina's murder as a blemish against his record.

The figure of Seneca is far more fully drawn; he is one whose style and manner Tacitus himself does not approve but who, nonetheless, mirrors the taste and learning of his age. The philosopher who lived the life of the opulent noble, with wealth unsurpassed by any not intimately connected with the imperial household, is a figure who has ever since his day drawn enthusiastic support and vigorous rebuke. On the whole Tacitus considers him only as a political figure; and his judgment here is, generally, inclined to be unfavorable, although sympathetic. In spite of that, Tacitus describes Seneca's end brilliantly and permits the old man to die with dignity and pride.

Thrasea, like Seneca a Stoic sage but otherwise totally different, is a man of unbending character and principle who, nonetheless, does not invoke blind resistance. It is not Thrasea so much as his less scrupulous followers who merit Tacitus's scorn as expressed in the *Agricola* about those martyrs who gained fame by an ostentatious death which served no public good. Tacitus's hero in the Nero books is obviously Thrasea. Yet there is one other person who is presented fully and sympathetically, and that is Corbulo because he was the greatest general of the day and the one closest to the *imperatores* of Rome's expansionist past.

In the treatment of character, one of the points that Tacitus often raises is the man's capability of rule. It is a significant part of the presentation even of lesser figures like Marcus Lepidus and Asinius Gallus. Until the year of the four emperors there was little chance that anyone not connected with the Julio–Claudian family could claim the purple. But once the secret of empire was out that an emperor could be made elsewhere than in Rome, anyone could hope that the power would fall to him. Writing in the days of Trajan, who had gained supreme rule just as had Galba and Vespasian, one might say, Tacitus clearly looked back over the first one and a third centuries of the empire to consider what men, who never had the chance, might have been good emperors, who, unlike Galba, not only were considered worthy of rule, but

would have proven to be so. What was the particular require-
ment that Tacitus would have imposed upon all emperors?

The answer to this large question lies, I think, in the *Agricola*, when Domitian broods over the prestige that the governor of Britain had obtained by his momentous victory at
Mons Graupius (39,2): *id sibi maxime formidolosum, privati hominis nomen supra principem adtolli: frustra studia
fori et civilium artium decus in silentium acta, si militarem
gloriam alius occuparet; cetera utcumque facilius dissimulari,
ducis boni imperatoriam virtutem esse* ("This was of particular concern to him, that the name of a subject was raised
above the emperor's: in vain had public eloquence and the
prestige of political careers been crushed and silenced, if someone else should lay claim to military glory; other talents were
rather easily disregarded, one way or another, but to be a good
general was the mark of an emperor"). Here is the key, *ducis
boni imperatoriam virtutem esse*. Who were the great generals who, like Vespasian and Trajan, might have become
emperor had adoption been the means of succession?

Agricola is the most obvious answer. History might have
offered an emperor from Gallia Narbonensis before it recorded one from Spain. Agricola and Trajan were contemporaries, but Agricola was the senior on every count: some
thirteen years older, consul fourteen years earlier, with experience in a martial province and a military reputation unri-
valled. Agricola had been made a patrician by Vespasian, who
clearly recognized in the younger man one like himself; he
possessed *auctoritas, vigor, constantia,* and an *expertus bellis
animus,* which shone all the more because of the *temeritas*
and *ignavia* of many other generals. Tacitus's description of
Vespasian's military virtues in the *Histories* could easily be
transferred to Agricola in the biography.

Mucianus, in his vigorous charge to Vespasian to claim the
empire, cites Corbulo as a potential rival to Nero, as Vespasian
was to Vitellius, who was murdered as a precaution by the
emperor. Corbulo plays a leading role in three books of the
Annals, and the picture of him that is presented is consistent
and cumulative. He was a general of the old school, clearly a
source of concern to Claudius (*formidolosum paci virum*

insignem et ignavo principi praegravem, Ann. XI:19,3).
Formidolosum is the crucial word; Domitian had taken Agricola's prestige ill (*id sibi maxime formidolosum, privati hominis nomen supra principem adtolli*). Corbulo ranked himself with the great generals of old when, in dismay upon being ordered to withdraw from Germany, he exclaimed, "*beatos quondam duces Romanos*" (XI:20,1), "Happy the Roman generals of old," and when he thought the recovery of Armenia, the conquest of Lucullus and Pompey, *dignum magnitudine populi Romani* (XIII:34,2), worthy of the grandeur of the Roman people. He was a *dux egregius* whose appointment to the Armenian command seemed to the Senate to have opened the way to ability (*locus virtutibus patefactus*). He displayed the accustomed qualities of a great general in the field and on the march, spoke with *auctoritas* which served him for eloquence, and was respected and trusted among Rome's enemies. A man of such talents and personal attributes clearly outshone the two emperors whom he served, one of whom blunted his military aspirations; the other, after using him in moments of crisis for the commonwealth, put him to death. Rome's greatest man for about a score of years, he was clearly one of Tacitus's heroes, and a man above all *capax imperii*.

His chief rival in prestige was not either of the emperors, but the only man who could challenge him for consideration as Rome's greatest marshal. This was Suetonius Paulinus, who subdued Mauretania at the beginning of Claudius's reign and later, as governor of Britain, withstood the revolt under the leadership of Boudicca. He was a *diligens ac moderatus dux*, gifted with *mira constantia* during the British crisis, who preferred slow and carefully planned campaigns to the uncertainties of speed and chance. *Ratio* and *cunctatio* combined to produce *auctoritas*. He had only one major shortcoming, and that was a vindictive arrogance toward those who surrendered after Boudicca's defeat. This lack of compassion kept the island in turmoil and led to his recall. Nonetheless, in the fateful year of the four emperors that saw Vespasian ultimately succeed to the mantle of the Caesars, it was Suetonius Paulinus whose military repute was the greatest of all, Corbulo now being dead. While serving Otho, he fancied that circumstances might lead the Senate to choose a new emperor and that he might be their choice, *quod vetustissimus consularium et militia clarus gloriam nomenque Britannicis expeditionibus meruisset* (*Hist.* II:37,1), "on the ground that he was the senior among the men of consular rank, that he was well known as a soldier, and had attained great distinction and fame by his campaigns in Britain."

Of Verginius Rufus little need be, or can be, said. He had the opportunity but resisted, whether because of lack of confidence in his own background or abilities or a sincere belief in the Senate's right to choose Nero's successor. He died at an advanced age in the year of Tacitus's consulate, having survived the years of decline under the Flavians and having reached the pinnacle of a third consulate as colleague of the emperor Nerva. It was Tacitus who delivered the eulogy at the funeral. He obviously knew and admired Verginius, but we cannot be sure whether he considered him material for the principate; he makes Valens say, when enflaming Vitellius's ambition, *merito dubitasse Verginium equestri familia, ignoto patre, imparem, si recepisset imperium, tutum, si recusasset* (*Hist.* I:52,4), ("It was well for Verginius to hesitate, the scion of a mere Equestrian family, and son of a father unknown to fame: he would have been unequal to empire, had he accepted it, and yet been safe though he refused it.") May we perhaps see a judgment on Verginius not unlike that on Galba, *omnium consensu capax imperii, nisi imperasset?* As it was, Verginius became a legend in his own lifetime with *admiratio* and *fama* even among those who hated him.

Nor was Mucianus quite good enough. Not unlike Petronius and Otho, he possessed a character marked by great virtues and great vices. He chose, probably because he realized his shortcomings, to make an emperor rather than to attempt to become emperor himself. His services to the cause of Vespasian were great; the Flavians profited from his undoubted abilities in civil administration; he himself became wealthy and gained a second and third consulate at very brief intervals from his first. But he had been too much concerned with his own prestige and military repute in the Italian campaign, and his arrogance offended the Senate. His arrival in Rome did not offer the commonwealth a respite from its sufferings under

Otho and Vitellius, only a change of characters: *donec successere Mucianus et Marcellus et magis alii homines quam alii mores* (*Hist.* II:95,3). A great general need not be *gloriae avidus atque omne belli decus sibi retinens* (III:8,3), "greedy of glory, and anxious to keep the whole credit of the war to himself," and he will lead men by the force of his own example and integrity. This Mucianus could not do.

Petilius Cerialis too falls short. Tacitus speaks favorably of his achievements in Britain in the early seventies, but his earlier career was chequered. He had been routed by Boudicca's forces because of *temeritas;* his rise in the turmoil of civil war was due more, perhaps, to his relationship with Vespasian than to his military renown, though he was not *inglorius militiae.* His actions were marked by bravado, his self-discipline was not all that it should have been (a commander should not absent himself from camp when the enemy is at hand to enjoy feminine attractions), and his preparations were careless and often impromptu (*sane Cerialis parum temporis ad exsequenda imperia dabat, subitus consiliis et eventu clarus: aderat fortuna, etiam ubi artes defuissent: hinc ipsi exercituique minor cura disciplinae, Hist.* V:21,3), "Cerialis in fact allowed too little time for executing his commands; he was hasty in his plans, though eminently successful in their results. Fortune helped him even where skill had failed, and so both the general and his army became less careful about discipline." Nonetheless, it is to Cerialis that Tacitus assigns the great justification of Rome's empire (*Hist.* IV:73–74), and his overall prestige is high.

Sextus Julius Frontinus is hardly mentioned in Tacitus's writings as we now have them. One may suspect that he would have played a significant role in the lost books of the *Histories.* In the *Agricola* (17,2), after speaking of Cerialis's achievement, Tacitus says, *et Cerialis quidem alterius successoris curam famamque obruisset: subiit sustinuitque molem Iulius Frontinus, vir magnus quantum licebat,* "And indeed Cerialis would have eclipsed the administration and reputation of any other successor, but Julius Frontinus, a great man as far as one could be great, took over and met the challenge." This is unusual praise; is the word *molem* to gain significance from its later use in the *Annals* (I:11,1), when Tiberius claims that only the capacity of Augustus had been equal to the burden of empire, *solam divi Augusti mentem tantae molis capacem? Vir magnus quantum licebat.* How great, indeed, had further opportunity been permitted? Pliny speaks of him in later years as *princeps vir.* Tacitus certainly got to know him well when their political careers intertwined and Frontinus crowned his career with a third consulate. Might Tacitus also, if we had his pages, have spoken of Frontinus as *princeps vir,* but with the added sense of *capax imperii?*

We thus conclude our inquiry. There are many others of whom Tacitus writes favorably, but none of them ranks as a potential emperor. For Tacitus, to maintain the well-being of the empire that he accepts, the emperor should be chosen from among the best, and the prime attribute must be military ability and repute. He must not be a *princeps proferendi imperi incuriosus* (*Ann.* IV:32,2), an emperor unconcerned with expansion of the empire. And, of the hundreds of individuals who fill Tacitus's narrative, only four stand out as *privati* who were *capaces imperii:* Corbulo, Suetonius Paulinus, Frontinus, and Agricola.

To sum up, Tacitus presents characters in two different ways, which we may call direct and indirect characterization. With the former he introduces an individual with a detailed description of his life and character, as with Sejanus and Poppaea Sabina, and then permits the remainder of the narrative to reveal the truth of his judgment. The reader knows from the beginning what the outcome of the individual's actions will be, causing prosperity or disaster. Similarly, the use of obituary enables Tacitus to recapitulate a life and career, thereby drawing together a number of threads that individually may have seemed negligible. Such is his final judgment on Marcus Lepidus (*Ann.* VI:27), the climax of a series of comments clearly showing Tacitus's great regard for him. More effective, however, is use of indirect characterization, and most of the major figures are permitted to show themselves over an extended period; it is their actions and words, rather than the historian's verdict, which mark them for good or ill. Seneca and Thrasea Paetus exemplify this approach.

Tacitus's treatment of character is such that the individual not only develops within himself but also frequently in interplay with others. Antonius Primus we know by himself. Tiberius we know better from his relations with the Senate and the members of his family than we ever could from a simple statement such as that made about Antonius. And many individuals who may perhaps represent types are, nonetheless, real because there are no two characters in Tacitus who can be precisely equated with each other. But there are some whose real impact is less personal than typical as, for example, many of the *delatores*, the informers. Few stand out by and of themselves, but the total impact caused by their participation in the increasing parade of trials for *maiestas*, treason, is powerful and grim.

Unquestionably, there are shortcomings in Tacitus's presentation of individuals. He fails to recognize that character is not set at birth and that human beings can change during the course of a lifetime. He seeks and presents an unvarying pattern, often failing to note that different circumstances will evoke differing responses without compromising the character of the person. Modern psychology has advanced beyond the limits of knowledge of human behavior recognized in antiquity; in this regard, as in so many others, Tacitus is the child, if not the victim, of his age. Yet, although his conclusions on the characters of individuals may not in every instance be fully valid, it is his great merit to have attempted to explain the events of state on the basis of human actions, and these actions on the basis of the characters of those responsible. All his characters are literary products, but the reader recognizes them as real people.

When Tacitus wields his pen to draw characters, he is concerned to produce individuals who will live, but not on a stage of no import. It is the drama of empire in which they move, and it is their relationship for good or ill to that empire, the well-being of the Roman people, and the prestige, nay survival, of the senatorial order that weigh most heavily in his personal judgment.

VIII. POLITICAL THOUGHT

What made Rome great was her freedom from internal stasis; so judged Polybius in an acute analysis of the workings of the Roman state which appears in his narrative at perhaps the most despondent juncture in Rome's history. But even while Polybius was writing, the seeds of internal discord and the beginning of the decline of the republic were being sown. The reason, to Sallust's mind, was the removal of salutary *metus hostilis*, fear of an enemy, with the destruction of Carthage, a *metus* that had kept Rome honest. This judgment is not in every respect accurate; there were instances of the breakdown of Roman *fides* before 146, but it is true that after that year Rome's outlook toward empire changed, and the ruling class thought less and less of their responsibility in government as a *patrocinium orbis*, a protectorate of the world. Soon after the proud triumph of the second Africanus over Rome's most feared opponent, Carthage was succeeded by a more dread enemy in the struggle against Roman supremacy, Romans themselves. The century of the Roman revolution was at hand.

> When the world had been subdued, when all rival kings and cities had been destroyed, and men had leisure to covet wealth which they might enjoy in security, the early conflicts between the patricians and the people were kindled into

flame. At one time the tribunes were factious, at another the consuls had unconstitutional power; it was in the capital and the forum that we first essayed civil wars. Then rose C. Marius, sprung from the very dregs of the populace, and L. Sulla, the most ruthless of the patricians, who perverted into absolute dominion the liberty which had yielded to their arms. After them came Cn. Pompeius, with a character more disguised but no way better. Henceforth men's sole object was supreme power.

This is one brief presentation of the last hundred years of the *res publica libera,* "the free republic," as it tends to be called. Nor is this all; our author elsewhere speaks of the Gracchi and Saturninus as *turbatores plebis,* "rabble-rousers," and Livius Drusus is no better. Sulla produced a respite, but not for long, and the consequence was that in a most corrupt state there was a superabundance of legislation (*corruptissima re publica plurimae leges*).

He continues: "Cneius Pompeius was then for the third time elected consul to reform public morals, but in applying remedies more terrible than the evils and repealing the legislation of which he had himself been the author, he lost by arms what by arms he had been maintaining. Then followed twenty years of continuous strife; custom or law there was none— *non mos, non ius;* the vilest deeds went unpunished, while many noble acts brought ruin."

This might, of course, come from Sallust were one not alert to the times covered which go beyond the boundaries of his monographs. We have here rather the bitter judgments of Tacitus, who has so often been called a devotee of the lost republic and who twisted the presentations of characters because he hated the positions they held, rather than because of the men they were. These passages (*Hist.* II:38 and *Ann.* III:27–28), referring to the late republic, are Sallustian in style and intended to evoke Sallust.

It is clear that Tacitus is not enthusiastic about the principate and emperors in the gloomy pages of the *Annals.* He may well, late in life, have yearned for the fresher days of the late republic before an oppressive oneness had cast its pall over the political scene. Yet one needs to remember that he himself served as a high functionary in imperial government, reaching the peaks of a consulate and governorship in the province of Asia and membership in one of the major priesthoods. Not for him was opposition to the principate, and I do not think that he was a hypocrite, who believed and wrote one thing but belied his beliefs in his actions.

Tacitus's purpose in writing history is unquestionably complex; there are certain themes that run through his works like threads. He is much concerned with *virtus*, personal excellence, and its survival under pressure. Indeed, this may be his prime purpose, for he says (*Ann.* III:65,1), *Exsequi sententias haud institui nisi insignes per honestum aut notabili dedecore, quod praecipuum munus annalium reor, ne virtutes sileantur utque pravis dictis factisque ex posteritate et infamia metus sit.* "My purpose is not to relate at length every motion, but only such as were conspicuous for excellence or notorious for infamy. This I regard as history's highest function, to let no worthy action be uncommemorated, and to hold out the reprobation of posterity as a terror to evil words and deeds."

Tacitus's philosophical belief in *virtus* never wavered. It was most readily observed in moments of crisis, and was present in women as well as men, in the meanest of social state and the proudest. A woman resisted the most terrible tortures after the revelation of the Pisonian conspiracy and refused to give information and betray another; men of high status were eager to save their own skins by involving others (*Ann.* XV:57).

> Nero, meanwhile, remembering that Epicharis was in custody on the information of Volusius Proculus, and assuming that a woman's frame must be unequal to the agony, ordered her to be torn on the rack. But neither the scourge nor fire, nor the fury of the men as they increased the torture that they might not be a woman's scorn, overcame her positive denial of the charge. Thus the first day's inquiry was futile. On the morrow, as she was being dragged back on a chair to the same torments (for with her limbs all dislocated she could not stand), she tied a band, which she had stript off her bosom, in a sort of noose to the arched back of the chair, put her neck in it, and then straining with the whole weight of her body, wrung out of her frame its little remaining breath. All the nobler was the example set by a freedwoman

at such a crisis in screening strangers and those whom she hardly knew, when freeborn men, Roman knights, and senators, yet unscathed by torture, betrayed, every one, his dearest kinsfolk.

Nor was there variation in his views on *libertas*, personal liberty, which in his age perhaps meant, most particularly, freedom of speech. In the principate of Trajan, it was a rare blessing to think what one wanted and to say what one thought (*Hist.* 1:1,4). Tacitus always admired those who had the courage of their convictions, men such as Thrasea Paetus, but nowhere indicated his championship of the right of men to speak and write according to their beliefs more than in the distinguished speech of Cremutius Cordus, charged with treason, *maiestas* (*Ann.* IV:34–35).

In the year of the consulship of Cornelius Cossus and Asinius Agrippa, Cremutius Cordus was arraigned on a new charge, now for the first time heard. He had published a history in which he had praised Marcus Brutus and called Caius Cassius the last of the Romans. His accusers were Satrius Secundus and Pinarius Natta, creatures of Sejanus. This was enough to ruin the accused; and then too the emperor listened with an angry frown to his defence, which Cremutius, resolved to give up his life, began thus:—

"It is my words, Senators, which are condemned, so innocent am I of any guilty act; yet these do not touch the emperor or the emperor's mother, who are alone comprehended under the law of treason. I am said to have praised Brutus and Cassius, whose careers many have described and no one mentioned without eulogy. Titus Livius, pre-eminently famous for eloquence and truthfulness, extolled Cneius Pompeius in such a panegyric that Augustus called him Pompeianus, and yet this was no obstacle to their friendship. Scipio, Afranius, this very Cassius, this same Brutus, he nowhere describes as brigands and traitors, terms now applied to them, but repeatedly as illustrious men. Asinius Pollio's writings too hand down a glorious memory of them, and Messala Corvinus used to speak with pride of Cassius as his general. Yet both these men prospered to the end with wealth and preferment. Again, that book of Marcus Cicero, in which he lauded Cato to the skies, how else was it answered by Caesar the dictator, than by a written oration in reply, as if he was pleading in court? The letters of Antonius, the harangues of Brutus contain reproaches against Augustus, false indeed, but urged with powerful sarcasm; the poems which we read of Bibaculus and Catullus are crammed with invectives on the Caesars. Yet the Divine Julius, the Divine Augustus themselves bore all this and let it pass, whether in forbearance or in wisdom I cannot easily say. Assuredly what is despised is soon forgotten; when you resent a thing, you seem to recognise it.

"Of the Greeks I say nothing; with them not only liberty, but even license went unpunished, or if a person aimed at chastising, he retaliated on satire by satire. It has, however, always been perfectly open to us without any one to censure, to speak freely of those whom death has withdrawn alike from the partialities of hatred or esteem. Are Cassius and Brutus now in arms on the fields of Philippi, and am I with them rousing the people by harangues to stir up civil war? Did they not fall more than seventy years ago, and as they are known to us by statues which even the conqueror did not destroy, so too is not some portion of their memory preserved for us by historians? To every man posterity gives his due honour, and, if a fatal sentence hangs over me, there will be those who will remember me as well as Cassius and Brutus."

He then left the Senate and ended his life by starvation. His books, so the Senators decreed, were to be burnt by the aediles; but some copies were left which were concealed and afterwards published. And so one is all the more inclined to laugh at the stupidity of men who suppose that the despotism of the present can actually efface the remembrances of the next generation. On the contrary, the persecution of genius fosters its influence; foreign tyrants, and all who have imitated their oppression, have merely procured infamy for themselves and glory for their victims.

Granted that Tacitus's views on themes of high import such as *virtus* and *libertas* were unswerving, it does not necessarily follow that his political outlook underwent no change during his lifetime as exemplified in his writings. I should here like to examine Tacitus's political thought and philosophy by two diverse means: first by an examination of his use of the words *principatus*, *dominatio*, and *regnum*, since mood and meaning can to a great extent be produced by choice of vocabulary, particularly in the case of words which are somewhat synonomous but which can have ominous overtones, then by a consideration of passages from Tacitus's entire corpus taken chronologically to ascertain whether there was any development in his thought.

The three short works may be examined together; only the first is significant in our context. *Principatus* is used three times in the *Agricola* (3,1; 7,2; 43,2), the first instance being the famed statement of the achievement of the new order by Nerva and Trajan, the reconciliation of two previously incompatible concepts, the principate and personal liberty. It is unquestionable, it appears, that this first statement must be considered as representative of Tacitus's thoughts about the form of government then in existence. Free men can live under it, and good men can find scope for their own advancement, the satisfaction of their *dignitas;* Trajan himself is a prime example of such a man. The government described is that set up by Augustus, *nomine principis*, and implies constitutionality. So too is the sense in the next use of the word. Different is the third instance: *ceterum per omnem valetudinem eius crebrius quam ex more principatus per nuntios visentis*, describing Domitian's frequent inquiries about the state of Agricola's health. In the context of the bitterness, sham, and deceit which have been described in the preceding chapters, the word here has evil connotations, but it might well be no more than a synonym for *princeps.*

The *Germany* has no instances of the use of *principatus*, as is to be expected in an ethnographic work dealing with a people too unsophisticated for such a form of government. The *Dialogue* offers two instances (17,3 and 6), both in the same chapter and both used in the same general sense of the form of government; the first gains a good tone, if anything, from the use in a relative clause of the verb *fovet.*

Dominatio, absent in the *Germany* and *Dialogue*, is twice hurled against the Romans in reproach by Calgacus to describe their rule over other peoples (30,2;32,1). It is not a term here appropriate for internal politics. Nor is *regnum*, which in the *Germany* refers to barbarian kingdoms and in the *Dialogue* has no political sense.

It is the *Histories* which enable us to gain insight into Tacitus's political mind. He uses all three words with careful distinction. *Regnum* is limited, with one dreadful exception, to the description of barbarian realms; *principatus* and *dominatio* begin to be paired in opposition to each other. The general sense which will also be found later in the *Annals* is here presented: the former is basically a neutral word and suggests good government, the latter is a Platonic perversion.

> *Quod si vita suppeditet, principatum divi Nervae et imperium Traiani, uberiorem securioremque materiam, senectuti seposui, rara temporum felicitate, ubi sentire quae velis et quae sentias dicere licet.*

> I have reserved as an employment for my old age, should my life be long enough, a subject at once more fruitful and less anxious in the reign of the Divine Nerva and the empire of Trajan, enjoying the rare happiness of times, when we may think what we please, and express what we think.

So writes Tacitus in the first chapter of the *Histories*. The mood recalls that of *Agricola* 3,1 written, probably, five or more years before the present passage. The feeling about the principate is still a balanced one; when the *princeps* is good, the form of government is good. The union of *principatus* and *imperium* is comparable to the pairings of *principatus* with *libertas* and with *consulatus; libertas* existed in the old republic under the *imperium* of the consuls. The good days of Trajan strongly differ from the terror of Domitian. Tacitus was not at this point of his historical writing able to attack the principate either in concept or in fact since, after all, he had been a functionary of it, with his career spanning the entire Flavian period, considering both his status as a senator beginning with the quaestorship and the minor posts preceding it.

After Galba had gained power, *potentia principatus divisa in Titum Vinium consulem, Cornelium Laconem praetorii praefectum; nec minor gratia Icelo Galbae liberto* (1:13,1), "the real power of the Empire was divided between T. Vinius, the consul, and Cornelius Laco, prefect of the Praetorian Guard. Icelus, a freedman of Galba, was in equal favour."

Potentia is a disparaging word which debases *principatus*, for influence is in the hands of subordinates who rise above their position. The word recalls the statement about Maecenas and Sallustius Crispus in *Ann.* III:30,3. Men such as these were powers behind the throne. Laco will surely call to mind the notorious Tigellinus, Nero's Sejanus, Icelus the heyday of Claudius's freedmen; neither of these recollections will be comforting.

In almost every other instance of its use in the *Histories*, *principatus* represents what is its prime sense in Tacitus, the literal meaning of the form of government under the guidance of one man. Nothing ill is meant, nothing ill is implied. Not that other interpretations beyond the simple statement are not also possible. Vitellius's division of labor among his staff is strongly contrasted with Galba's actions: *igitur laudata militum alacritate Vitellius ministeria principatus per libertos agi solita in equites Romanos disponit* (1:58,1), "Vitellius, after bestowing high commendation on the zeal of the soldiers, proceeded to distribute among Roman Knights the offices of the Imperial court usually held by freedmen."

In 1:77,1 *sic distractis exercitibus ac provinciis Vitellio quidem ad capessendam principatus fortunam bello opus erat*, "As the armies and provinces were thus divided, Vitellius, in order to secure the sovereign power, was compelled to fight," the expression perhaps recalls the obituary of Galba, *capax imperii*, with the same proviso, *nisi imperasset*, although the picture of Vitellius which has been painted thus far is of a slothful man; the attempt to reign will be his downfall.

Principatus gains a pejorative sense by being linked with *invidia* in a phrase which Tacitus reworked in the *Annals: magna cum invidia novi principatus, cuius hoc primum specimen noscebatur* (11:64,1), "great odium upon the new reign, and was noted as the first indication of its character." In *Ann.* 1:6 and XIII:1 the same kind of thought is expressed with greater directness and power, and by its position at the beginning of the chapter is strongly underscored. Again, Blaesus is shown to have been, in a way, more fortunate than Galba, by having kept the reputation of being *capax imperii: sanctus inturbidus, nullius repentini honoris, adeo non principatus adpetens, parum effugerat ne dignus crederetur* (III:39,2), "A righteous man and a lover of peace, who coveted no sudden elevation, much less the throne, he could not escape being thought to deserve it."

Dominatio is used six times in the *Histories*, compared with the thirty-two instances of *principatus*. The contrast is strong and intentional. It stands for unconstitutionality, either in office or the use of the powers of an office. Tacitus's excursus on earlier history is particularly illuminating (II:38):

> That old passion for power which has been ever innate in man increased and broke out as the Empire grew in greatness. In a state of moderate dimensions equality was easily preserved; but when the world had been subdued, when all rival kings and cities had been destroyed, and men had leisure to covet wealth which they might enjoy in security, the early conflicts between the patricians and the people were kindled into flame. At one time the tribunes were factious, at another the consuls had unconstitutional power; it was in the capital and the forum that we first essayed civil wars. Then rose C. Marius, sprung from the very dregs of the populace, and L. Sulla, the most ruthless of the patricians, who perverted into absolute dominion the liberty which had yielded to their arms. After them came Cn. Pompeius, with a character more disguised but no way better. Henceforth men's sole object was supreme power. Legions formed of Roman citizens did not lay down their arms at Pharsalia and Philippi, much less were the armies of Otho and Vitellius likely of their own accord to abandon their strife. They were driven into civil war by the same wrath from heaven, the same madness among men, the same incentives to crime. That these wars were terminated by what we may call single blows, was owing to want of energy in the chiefs. But these reflections on the character of ancient and modern times have carried me too far from my subject. I now return to the course of events.

The language is very similar to that of the first chapter of the *Annals*. *Libertas* is perverted into *dominatio*, the rule of one man without limitation of power or lust, without check by the state; *potentia*, normally based upon arms or illicit influence, has its place in both passages. The progression will follow a course such as this: the *libertas* of all is perverted into personal *dominatio* by *cupido potentiae*, which is then overthrown by a *princeps*, who in turn restores *libertas*, although the change of definition of liberty must be kept in mind. It was first connected with the consul, later with the princeps; if the princeps is an unworthy man, there is a return to *dominatio*, for which there is no cure save the death of the princeps and the succession of a better man.

The incompatibility of *libertas* and *dominatio* is underscored in IV:8,4: *quo modo pessimis imperatoribus sine fine dominationem, ita quamvis egregiis modum libertatis placere,* "for as the worst Emperors love an unlimited despotism, so the noblest like some check on liberty." The substitution of *imperator* for *princeps* was surely intentional; the reader will perhaps have thought of Jupiter's mighty statement of Rome's future (*Aeneid* 1:279): *imperium sine fine dedi,* "I have granted empire without end."

This incompatibility is clearly noted also in IV:73,3: *ceterum libertas et speciosa nomina praetexuntur; nec quisquam alienum servitium et dominationem sibi concupivit, ut non eadem ista vocabula usurparet,* "liberty, indeed, and the like specious names are their pretexts; but never did any man seek to enslave his fellows and secure dominion for himself, without using the very same words." *Dominatio* is defined as personal power without limit, which imposes slavery on all others and is the very antithesis of liberty. This quest for unconstitutional rule was characteristic of both Otho and Vitellius (I:36,3 and II:63,1).

These passages have been concerned with the internal political life of Rome. The final use of *dominatio* in the *Histories*, though referring to the Jews, sounds a warning for Rome as well: (*reges*) *mobilitate volgi expulsi, resumpta per arma dominatione fugas civium, urbium eversiones, fratrum coniugum parentum neces aliaque solita regibus ausi superstitionem fovebant, quia honor sacerdotii firmamentum potentiae adsumebatur* (V:8,3), "expelled by the fickle populace, and regaining their throne by force of arms, these princes, while they ventured on the wholesale banishment of their subjects, on the destruction of cities, on the murder of brothers, wives, and parents, and the other usual atrocities of despots, fostered the national superstition by appropriating the dignity of the priesthood as the support of their political power." The quest for personal power depends upon *potentia*; the *dominus* is equated with *rex*, a hateful and portentous word for Rome.

Tacitus meticulously avoids the use of *regnum* in the *His-*

tories in consideration of the Roman political climate, with one exception. This occurs early in the work, and serves as a dreadful indictment of Nero's reign; the sentence, contrary to Tacitus's customary style, is long and involved, and ends with one of his famous truisms.

> *Non erat Othonis mollis et corpori similis animus, et intimi libertorum servorumque, corruptius quam in privata domo habiti, aulam Neronis et luxus, adulteria matrimonia ceterasque regnorum libidines avido talium, si auderet, ut sua ostentantes, quiescenti ut aliena exprobrabant, urgentibus etiam mathematicis, dum novos motus et clarum Othoni annum observatione siderum adfirmant, genus hominum potentibus infidum, sperantibus fallax, quod in civitate nostra et vetabitur semper et retinebitur* (I:22,1).

The soul of Otho was not effeminate like his person. His confidential freedmen and slaves, who enjoyed a license unknown in private families, brought the debaucheries of Nero's court, its intrigues, its easy marriages, and the other indulgences of despotic power, before a mind passionately fond of such things, dwelt upon them as his if he dared to seize them, and reproached the inaction that would leave them to others. The astrologers also urged him to action, predicting from their observation of the heavens' revolutions, and a year of glory for Otho. This is a class of men, whom the powerful cannot trust, and who deceive the aspiring, a class which will always be proscribed in this country, and yet always retained.

The similarity of Nero and Otho is clear, and the aside about the astrologers will perhaps be recalled, years later, by the similar interests of Tiberius.

The excursus about the Jews at the beginning of Book v dates a migration of this people from Crete to Libya, *qua tempestate Saturnus vi Iovis pulsus cesserit regnis* (v:2,1), "about the time when Saturn was driven from his throne by the power of Jupiter." Here too is a reminiscence of Vergil and his *Saturnia regna*. *Regnum* is used eleven other times, always with reference to barbarian kingdoms, which is the proper meaning and scope of the word.

From the evidence of the *Histories*, then, it seems clear that Tacitus's view of the principate is still a sanguine one; there has been no disillusion which will conflict with the hopeful expressions of the *Agricola*. His regular word for the government is *principatus*, used thirty-two times, its meaning clear and precise. *Dominatio*, used only six times, represents the perversion of good government; *regnum*, which appears thirteen times, has negligible reference to Rome. The transition in time and experience, from *Histories* to *Annals*, is marked by a change in mood and a change of emphasis. The proportions of the use of these words are diametrically reversed.

In the first chapter of the *Annals*, Tacitus presents his program: *inde consilium mihi pauca de Augusto et extrema tradere, mox Tiberii principatum et cetera, sine ira et studio, quorum causas procul habeo*, "hence my purpose is to relate a few facts about Augustus—more particularly his last acts, then the reign of Tiberius, and all which follows, without either bitterness or partiality, from any motives to which I am far removed." *Principatus* stands for the accepted and legal term for the form of government, as generally in the *Histories*. Tacitus is not yet ready to bring about a change in connotation, but the suggestions come very soon.

Primum facinus novi principatus fuit Postumi Agrippae caedes (1:6,1). "The first crime of the new reign was the murder of Postumus Agrippa." Nothing is said to indicate that the principate is of itself bad; but its close relation with *facinus*, itself a word originally neutral but at this time, and long since, evil, in a word order emphasized by synchysis, compels this interpretation. Later in the same chapter, Sallustius Crispus reminds Livia of the requirements of empire: *monuit Liviam, ne arcana domus, ne consilia amicorum, ministeria militum vulgarentur, neve Tiberius vim principatus resolveret cuncta ad senatum vocando: eam condicionem esse imperandi, ut non aliter ratio constet quam si uni reddatur*, "he advised Livia not to divulge the secrets of her house or the counsels of friends, or any services performed by the soldiers, nor to let Tiberius weaken the strength of imperial power by referring everything to the Senate, for 'the condition,' he said, 'of holding empire is that an account cannot be balanced unless it be rendered to one person.'" Repetition of *principatus* at the end of a chapter so ominously begun, and here joined with elements of secrecy, *arcana* and *vulgarentur*, cannot fail to give it a pejorative sense.

In the following chapter *principatus* is found for the last time in the *Annals* in the neutral, descriptive sense. Thereafter, a value judgment is always attached. Tiberius sends instructions to the armies as if he had received the principate, i.e. become *princeps* (1:7,5). In III:28,2, the word *princeps*, perhaps used as a synonym for *principatus*, is joined with *pax*. This collocation is uplifting, but the following words dampen the reader's emotions; this too is the effect of the use of the word *potentia*. *Caesar Augustus, potentiae securus, quae triumviratu iusserat abolevit deditque iura, quis pace et principe uteremur. acriora ex eo vincla:* "Caesar Augustus, feeling his power secure, annulled the decrees of his triumvirate, and gave us a constitution which might serve us in peace under a monarchy. Henceforth our chains became more galling." In the year 22, as Tacitus approaches the end of the first half of the first hexad, Tiberius is consolidating his power: *Sed Tiberius, vim principatus sibi firmans* (III:60,1), while affecting the importance and independence of the Senate. The relationship with power is underscored; *vis* is either good or bad, but recollection of 1:6 will emphasize the latter. The introduction to Book IV is here forecast, when everything became topsy-turvy under the influence of the evil spirit Sejanus (*cum repente turbare fortuna coepit, saevire ipse aut saevientibus vires praebere*). Tacitus leaves no doubt about this change, which marks the year A.D. 23: *quoniam Tiberio mutati in deterius principatus initium ille annus attulit* (IV:6,1). After this *principatus* appears no more in the *Annals* save to mark the beginning of Nero's reign. The perverted principate (*in deterius mutatus*) has degenerated into *dominatio* and *regnum*. The unmitigatedly evil years of Tiberius have now begun.

The parallel progression of the periods of Tiberius and Nero is underscored at the beginning of the thirteenth book: *prima novo principatu mors Iunii Silani proconsulis Asiae ignaro Nerone per dolum Agrippinae paratur*, "the first death under the new emperor, that of Junius Silanus, proconsul of Asia, was, without Nero's knowledge, planned by the treachery of Agrippina." This paraphrases 1:6,1. Nero is said to have been ignorant of the deed, as Tiberius claimed to be of Agrippa's death. And is there in the treachery of Agrippina a hint at the complicity, or sole responsibility, of Livia in the murder of Augustus's grandson?

As Tiberius's first nine years in office were on the whole good, so too was the period at the beginning of Nero's reign, sometimes known as the *quinquennium*, under the influence of Seneca and Burrus. Nero claims for himself the respect due a true *princeps* in his exposition of the future: *tum formam futuri principatus praescripsit, ea maxime declinans, quorum recens flagrabat invidia* (XIII:4,2), "he then sketched the plan of his future government, carefully avoiding anything which had kindled recent odium." All readers, familiar with the outcome of Nero's rule, will have snickered at the use of *principatus* here in its strict, almost forgotten sense of the form of government, which forecasts constitutional, if not good, government or, at the minimum, the absence of bad. This principate too will soon become changed *in deterius*.

One theme of the *Annals* is the corruption of state, of people, of morals under a government dominated, not guided, by one man. For this state of affairs the crucial word is *dominatio*, the responsible man no longer *princeps* but *dominus*. Life under Domitian clearly revealed what that entailed. The word appears in the very first chapter of the *Annals*, describing the chaos of the years controlled by Cinna and Sulla; *potentia* follows closely, and the commonwealth, exhausted by the dynasts, can find rest only under a *princeps*. This is *per se* good, and this viewpoint is continued by use of the word *principatus* at the chapter's end; what intervenes is parenthetical.

But this mood is shattered almost at once. Augustus's plans for the succession look toward the continuation of his family's hegemony: *ceterum Augustus subsidia dominationi Claudium Marcellum* (I:3,1). The nature of this hegemony is shudderingly clear.

Tacitus's joining of *dominatio* with *arcana* in his description of the special status of Egypt (II:59,3) is doubly significant. The image of Augustus's principate was to him pure facade, based upon unreality and deception, and *arcana* has baleful political overtones.

The Sallustian character sketch of Sejanus prefaces his personal traits with a statement of his goal: *nunc originem mores et quo facinore dominationem raptum ierit, expediam* (IV:1,1), "I will now fully describe his extraction, his character, and the daring wickedness by which he grasped at power." The violent careers of Cinna and Sulla will come to mind. This too, according to the talk of her enemies, was the goal of Agrippina: *superbam fecunditate, subnixam popularibus studiis inhiare dominationi apud Caesarem arguerent* (IV:12,3), "(he urged both these women) to represent to the Emperor that her pride as a mother and her reliance on popular enthusiasm were leading her to dream of empire." She is thus no different from Sejanus; each seeks something illegal. She is now seeking the power, it is claimed, which, *mutatis mutandis*, Tiberius was afraid Germanicus might prefer to have at once rather than anticipate. Tiberius's relationships with his mother hinge greatly upon personal power and the resulting struggle between them for dominance over the other: *traditur etiam matris impotentia extrusum, quam dominationis sociam aspernabatur neque depellere poterat, cum dominationem ipsam donum eius accepisset* (IV:57,3), "according to one account his mother's domineering temper drove him away; he was weary of having her as his partner in power, and he could not thrust her aside, because he had received this very power as her gift." The use of the word *dominatio* twice within eight words is significant and delineates beyond doubt the nature of Tiberius's rule. Tacitus does not often repeat himself in this way.

In spite of the bitterness between the emperor and his mother, Tacitus felt that she was a restraining influence upon him. As Book IV had begun with the corruption of a basically good principate because of the ascendancy of Sejanus, so in Book V is this intensified. With Augusta dead, there is no one with influence opposed to Sejanus; within the state there is total chaos in constitutional processes: *ceterum ex eo praerupta iam et urgens dominatio* (V:3,1), "this at all events was the beginning of an unmitigated and grinding despotism."

The approach of death for Tiberius brings the rapid appearance of *dominatio* four times within seven chapters to serve as a pervading theme of his obituary. The first of these, although explicitly about Artabanus, carries general import: *nam populi imperium iuxta libertatem, paucorum dominatio regiae libidini propior est* (VI:42,2), "as a fact, popular government almost amounts to freedom, while the rule of the few approaches closely to a monarch's caprice." *Libertas* is paired, in contrast, with *dominatio*, as elsewhere supplementarily with *consulatus* and *principatus*. The expression has ancestry in Sallust's *factio paucorum*, and the implication is clear that *dominatio unius* is *regnum*. The next two instances are referred to Artabanus (VI:43,2) and Caligula (VI:45,3); the last is the final word in the Tiberius books to describe his reign: *an, cum Tiberius post tantam rerum experientiam vi dominationis convulsus et mutatus sit* (VI:48,2), "was it probable that, when Tiberius with his long experience of affairs was, under the influence of absolute power, wholly perverted and changed?" The concluding chapter (fifty-one) is concerned with personality.

Mood is less important in Books XI–XVI, since the nature of Claudius's and Nero's reigns is obvious. *Dominatio* three times refers to barbarian affairs as it had once in the first six books. Agrippina the Younger's naked lust for power is characterized by this word, which shows her to be the true daughter of her mother, and it forecasts what Nero's reign will be long before it is characterized as a *principatus* (XII:4,1; 7,3; 8,2). Soon thereafter (11,2), Claudius urges the Parthian Meherdates to establish in his country a government based on generosity and justice rather than a *dominatio;* this occurs at the very time that the *dominatio* of Agrippina and Nero is being prepared at Rome.

A passage at the beginning of Book XIII, part of which we have already noted, brings the perversion of *principatus* to its foregone conclusion: *prima novo principatu mors Iunii Silani proconsulis Asiae ignaro Nerone per dolum Agrippinae paratur, non quia ingenii violentia exitium inritaverat, segnis et dominationibus aliis fastiditus*, "the first death under the new emperor, that of Junius Silanus, proconsul of Asia, was, without Nero's knowledge, planned by the treachery of Agrippina. Not that Silanus had provoked destruction by any violence of temper, apathetic as he was, and so utterly despised under former despotisms." The junction of the two words is psychologically powerful; they appear in the first chapter of the whole work, but not so closely connected. Here the equation is clear: *principatus* is *dominatio*, and the master is a *dominus*.

Agrippina is stigmatized three more times with the charge that she sought a *dominatio;* the word describes the feelings of the Britons about Rome's rule, and Nero, *ad vim dominationis conversus*, "had recourse to the sheer might of despotism," despatching a tribune during the repression of the Pisonian conspiracy (XV:69,1). *Dominatio* is used no more in the *Annals* as we have them. Tacitus had no need to; he had made his point.

Of the numerous instances of the use of *regnum* in the *Annals*, sixty-two in all, only eight have direct reference to Rome; one more may be so interpreted. Its general purpose is to describe the form of government of other peoples. Tacitus specifically states that Augustus did not establish a kingdom or a dictatorship, but a principate (1:9,5); yet this contrast, clear at the time, was effectually blurred as decades passed. In general, however, the word is limited in use to those to whom unmitigated evil can be ascribed: to Sejanus, Agrippina, Nero, and less properly and directly Claudius.

The description of Sejanus which introduces Book IV concludes with the words *saepius industria ac vigilantia, haud minus noxiae, quotiens parando regno finguntur*, "oftener energetic and watchful, qualities quite as mischievous when hypocritically assumed for the attainment of sovereignty." He then wins over Livilla, the wife of Drusus: *ad coniugii spem, consortium regni et necem mariti impulit* (IV:3,3), "lured her on to thoughts of marriage, of a share in sovereignty, and of her husband's destruction." Tacitus's judgment of his goal is brutally clear. The word, it can be conjectured, would have reappeared in the pages dealing with the conspiracy and downfall of the minister.

Agrippina cherished wealth, not for its sake alone, but *quasi subsidium regno pararetur* (XII:7,3), "under the pretext that riches were being accumulated as a prop to the throne." The sentence preceding this one is marked by *dominatio*. The two words combine to emphasize her illegal aims, terrible in themselves, but made more so by the fact that she is a woman. Her ambition subordinated all things to itself: *ne quis ambigat decus pudorem corpus, cuncta regno viliora habere* (XII:65,2), "so that no one could doubt that she held honour, modesty and her very person, everything, in short, cheaper than sovereignty." To hasten Claudius's demise, *deligitur artifex talium vocabulo Locusta, nuper veneficii damnata et diu inter instrumenta regni habita* (XII:66,2), "a person skilled in such matters was selected, Locusta by name, who had lately been condemned for poisoning, and had long been retained as one of the tools of despotism." The dread import of the last phrase can be compared with *subsidia dominationi* (1:3,1) and *subsidium regno* which we have just considered.

Nero, at the beginning of his principate, outlined the constitutional framework which he proposed to follow. To emphasize the nature of his reign, he used the word *principatus;* and then he contrasted his regime with that of Claudius by his removal of Pallas from office: *demovet Pallantem cura rerum, quis a Claudio impositus velut arbitrium regni agebat* (XIII:14,1), "Nero removed Pallas from the charge of the business with which he had been entrusted by Claudius, and in which he acted, so to say, as the controller of the throne." His criticism of his adoptive father need not be taken seriously, and in fact the word *regnum* suggests how shallow his own claim was. Almost at once Tacitus does apply the word to him, in his discussion of public reaction to the murder of Britannicus: *cui plerique etiam hominum ignoscebant, antiquas fratrum discordias et insociabile regnum aestimantes* (XIII:17,1), "which many were even inclined to forgive when they remembered the immemorial feuds of brothers and the impossibility of a divided throne."

The passage with implied meaning deals with the condemnation of Barea Soranus: *tempus damnationi delectum, quo Tiridates accipiendo Armeniae regno adventabat* (XVI:23,2), "the time chosen for the fatal sentence was that at which Tiridates was on his way to receive the sovereignty of Armenia." The juxtaposition of Tiridates's *regnum* with the arbitrary action of Nero imposes the autocratic meaning of the former upon the latter.

This precise distinction in choice and use of words is an instance of Tacitus's artistic and intentional creation of mood.

He once accepted the principate, but maturity brought bitterness which could not be concealed in his history and which he did not want to conceal. It might have been too dangerous to be explicit, as Juvenal too realized, but there is no doubt that one of Tacitus's themes was the change from *principatus* to *dominatio*.

We turn now to our second undertaking, the examination of passages from Tacitus's entire output. There will be occasional overlapping and repetition with what has been said above, but this is intentional for the purposes of clarity and completeness. One must, of course, be cautious in attempting to extract the thoughts of an author from his works, particularly from a historian as brilliant as Tacitus in the production of speeches for his characters. Where does a figure in the narrative fairly represent the author? Surely it would be foolhardy, indeed wrong, to delineate Tacitus's views on empire on the basis of Calgacus's outburst in the *Agricola*, marked by the devastating *ubi solitudinem faciunt, pacem appellant*. Cerialis, in his reasoned defense of empire and the peace and stability that it brings (*Hist.* IV:73–74), must more fairly represent the senator, consul, and governor who wrote history with the knowledge of the workings of that empire. He, like his father-in-law and the reigning emperor, had chosen not to become part of the disloyal opposition but rather to serve the commonwealth. There is throughout Tacitus's work a tension between those who opposed the emperors and those who served them. Was he defending himself, among others, against insinuations of improper behavior when he cried out, late in the *Agricola* (42,4), *sciant, quibus moris est inlicita mirari, posse etiam sub malis principibus magnos viros esse, obsequiumque ac modestiam, si industria ac vigor adsint, eo laudis excedere, quo plerique per abrupta sed in nullum rei publicae usum ambitiosa morte inclaruerunt?* "Let those whose custom it is to admire actions that are forbidden know that great men can exist even under bad emperors; and allegiance and moderation, if hard work and vigorous action are added, can reach the same level of renown that many have reached by dangerous paths, but they became famous by an ostentatious death, with no advantage to the state."

Yet, if one wishes to determine what Tacitus thought about

empire, there is no alternative to dissection of the text, with the understanding that not all are likely to agree with everything.

There is to me no doubt that Tacitus's reception of the principate of Nerva and his adoption of Trajan were warmly enthusiastic and sincere. Early in the biography of his father-in-law, he speaks of the return of men's spirits and praises Nerva for having, at the very beginning of the *beatissimum saeculum*, reconciled the principate and individual liberty, which had formerly been incompatible (3,1), and late in the work he regrets that Agricola had not been allowed to survive into the light of the *beatissimum saeculum* and to see Trajan as emperor, which he had prayed for and forecast (44,5). Certainly, at this point, there is nothing wrong with the principate if there is the right kind of princeps, for the principate has not been responsible for a decline of Rome's prestige and power, even granting that not every princeps was interested in extending the empire (Tiberius, one will recall, was charged [*Ann.* IV:32,2] with being *proferendi imperi incuriosus*). When Tacitus says in the *Germany* (29,3), *protulit enim magnitudo populi Romani ultra Rhenum ultraque veteres terminos imperii reverentiam*, "for the greatness of the Roman people had extended respect for the empire beyond the Rhine and, in consequence, beyond its ancient boundaries," he refers not only to Domitian by circumlocution but to the stature of the Roman State before Domitian's reign as well; and the statement should be compared with that in the *Agricola* (23) where the Roman army was prevented from settling for boundaries this side of Scotland by their own bravery and the glory of the Roman name, *ac si virtus exercitus et Romani nominis gloria pateretur, inventus in ipsa Britannia terminus.*

Everything is not always better in the past and worse in the present, says Tacitus in the *Dialogue* (18,3). Our own age has much that is good which posterity could emulate. For history seems to follow a cyclical pattern; customs and practices change as do the seasons (*Ann.* III:55,5). The past had freedom and license, the present peace and order. The emperor is called *sapientissimus et unus* (Dial. 41,4). The empire is the *optimus civitatis status* (37,5), "the best kind of state."

How is this great and peaceful state to be gotten, how is it to be maintained? The key is, of course, the emperor. How will he be chosen? The answer is given in Galba's long speech on the adoption of Piso which, to my mind, perhaps represents Tacitus's own views more than anything else he ever wrote.

When Galba had assumed the purple as Nero's successor in the midst of violence and grumbling, he realized, because of his concern for the state, that the elimination of Nero would prove futile were the commonwealth to pass into the hands of Otho. He therefore adopted a young man of eminent family but lacking in the achievements and reputation necessary to weld a people together in a moment of crisis. This was Piso Licinianus, whose moments of glory were to be brief. Galba begins his address at the ceremony of adoption by expatiating on Piso's illustrious ancestry and his own; then, claiming that he himself had been summoned to power with the support of gods and men (*deorum hominumque consensu ad imperium vocatum, Hist.* 1:15,1), he offers the principate, in the past the prize of warfare, to his selected successor as the deified Augustus had sought his successor first in his nephew, then in his son-in-law, then in his grandsons, and finally in his stepson. But Augustus looked no further than his own household, Galba sought in the state, because there he was able to find the best man. Next comes the most crucial part of his discourse.

Could the vast frame of this empire have stood and preserved its balance without a directing spirit, I was not unworthy of inaugurating a republic. As it is, we have been long reduced to a position, in which my age can confer no greater boon on the Roman people than a good successor, your youth no greater than a good emperor. Under Tiberius, Caius, and Claudius, we were, so to speak, the inheritance of a single family. The choice which begins with us will be a substitute for freedom. Now that the family of the Julii and the Claudii has come to an end, adoption will discover the worthiest successor. To be begotten and born of a princely race is a mere accident, and is only valued as such. In adoption there is nothing that need bias the judgment, and if you wish to make a choice, an unanimous opinion points out the man.

The last few lines are crucial: *loco libertatis erit quod eligi coepimus; et finita Iuliorum Claudiorumque domo optimum quemque adoptio inveniet* (16,1). The state cannot exist without an emperor, but there cannot be full freedom or total enslavement (*imperaturus es hominibus, qui nec totam servitutem pati possunt nec totam libertatem*, 16,4). That being the case, the best method of choosing an emperor is not relation by blood but by adoption. There is unquestionable criticism of the descendants of Augustus and of Vespasian; without family connections, Gaius, Claudius, Nero, and Domitian would never have been emperors. Tiberius and Vespasian had long and distinguished careers behind them when, in the fullness of years, they clearly stood out above any potential rival; and Titus, though Vespasian's son, was on his own *capax imperii* (II:77). The only parallel with the adoption of Piso was that of Trajan by Nerva. Piso's choice was unwise and doomed, for, in spite of Galba's boast, he himself had not been the elect of gods and men. The omens were unfavorable for the presentation of Piso to the praetorians, but with Trajan the gods supported the choice—*he* was *divinitus constitutus princeps*. And there was something else; Trajan was a distinguished man with an outstanding career.

These statements seem to make it perfectly clear that Tacitus recognized the necessity for the principate and even was enthusiastic about it, provided the emperor was good. The accession of Nerva, followed very quickly by the adoption of Trajan, caused him to believe that stability of government and the opportunity for senators to pursue public careers could coexist; and his increasing gloom as his writing career advanced arose not from dissatisfaction with Trajan but from the realization that it is precisely under good emperors, particularly under an *optimus princeps*, that power tends to fall more and more into the hands of the ruler. In the last analysis he realized that the Senate must always be inferior to the emperor, even an emperor who respected the body from which he rose; as Otho said to the praetorians (1:84,4), "For you give the state its Senators, and the Senate gives it its Princes." But Tacitus did grant that there were good emperors (1:46,4); for that, one must be grateful, and to guarantee a good succession is perhaps the main responsibility of the current princeps. How important and how effective this could be is clearly illustrated by Rome's experience under the five "good" emperors, from Nerva to Marcus Aurelius, each of whom save the last adopted his successor.

What the empire has given must of course be balanced by what has been lost. This was the theme of Maternus's remarks in the *Dialogue;* it is continued in the speech of Curtius Montanus late in the surviving books of the *Histories* (IV:42,6): *non timemus Vespasianum: ea principis aetas, ea moderatio; sed diutius durant exempla quam mores. elanguimus, patres conscripti, nec iam ille senatus sumus, qui occiso Nerone delatores et ministros more maiorum puniendos flagitabat. optimus est post malum principem dies primus.* "We are not afraid of Vespasian; the age and moderation of the new Emperor reassure us. But the influence of an example outlives the individual character. We have lost our vigour, Conscript Fathers; we are no longer that Senate, which, when Nero had fallen, demanded that the informers and ministers of the tyrant should be punished according to ancient custom. The first day after the downfall of a wicked Emperor is the best of opportunities."

The importance of these words has recently been underscored by R. H. Martin, *Journal of Roman Studies,* LVII (1967): 114:

They are remarkably appropriate to the mood of a critical observer writing in the early years of Trajan's reign, when initial enthusiasm for the new emperor had begun to be replaced by a feeling of disillusionment. If behind these last words of Curtius Montanus we can see something of the thoughts of Cornelius Tacitus, it is scarcely too much to see . . . a palinode to what Tacitus had written in *Agricola* 3. There, while welcoming the new era of Nerva and Trajan in terms of some warmth, Tacitus had apologized for being unable to greet the new age with the immediate enthusiasm and upsurge of spirit it deserved; these things, he said, take time: destruction is instant, growth a slow process. In 98 that was something to look forward to. When Curtius Montanus' speech was written, time enough had elapsed to allow the spirits ravaged by the Domitianic terror to recover; the conclusion of Montanus' speech shows that those hopes had not been realized. Looking back over the intervening years Tacitus could observe that time had seen, not growth and improvement (*lente augescunt*, *Ag.* 3) but decline (*elanguimus*, *Hist.* IV:42). The best time was not to come: it was already past—*optimus est post malum principem dies primus*. Internal peace and settled government there was: great eloquence and political freedom, no.

Tacitus's mood is set; the *Annals* add nothing new. The dominant tone in his last work is one of acceptance with regret. The burden of the empire is so great that one man can scarcely meet it; yet there is no alternative, for the days of personal freedom had been destructive and that freedom largely elusive.

To be emperor required capacity that was almost superhuman. Even Tiberius, with his extraordinary background of public service, was overwhelmed by the weight of office (*post tantam rerum experientiam vi dominationis convulsus et mutatus*, *Ann.* VI:48,2); how could lesser men withstand it? Tiberius himself admitted his shortcomings, saying that he did not have the capacity of Augustus (*solam divi Augusti mentem tantae molis capacem*, *Ann.* I:11,1), and Mucianus aroused Vespasian's ambition by pointing out that he would challenge a Vitellius, not an Augustus (*non adversus divi Augusti acerrimam mentem*, *Hist.* II:76,2). To manage the empire was as difficult a task as it once had been for Aeneas to found the Roman people: *tantae molis erat Romanam condere gentem* (*Aen.* I:33). Vergil's *Romana gens* has become the equivalent, in Tacitus's mind, of the *imperium Romanum*.

The early *populus Romanus* was able to be well-ruled by consuls; but when the empire gradually evolved, the inadequacy of the city-state's capacity for government on a larger scale became obvious. Augustus brought peace; that was his greatest gift. For every gain there was a corresponding loss; Maternus's comments are repeated, on a larger scale, in the talk for and against Augustus after the emperor's death. No one really expected that the old republic would return, and the great majority would not have welcomed it. That being the case, *sic converso statu neque alia re Romana quam si unus imperitet* (*Ann.* IV:33,2), the real and crucial question was, who would that *unus* be? Tacitus's answers to this query have been indicated in the previous chapter.

The principate exists; late in the first century B.C., there had been no alternative, at least none that would have been better; nor would Tacitus, after the gloomy days of Domitian, have been willing to live under a different form of government, at least one that had a realistic, not an idealistic hope. If the emperor is good, all will be well, and *libertas* will not be crushed by *principatus*. The years of Trajan's reign showed that this was really an idle dream: the senatorial order may have freedom of speech and prestige, but power, meaningful power, is virtually nonexistent. Tacitus was embittered by this; he might, in his old age, have longed for something else, but that was not to be. The principate could easily turn to autocracy; one could do no more than hope for the best.

IX. HISTORICAL INTEGRITY

At the beginning of the *Histories* Tacitus says that he will write *neque amore et sine odio*, "without partiality and without hatred." Similarly, at the beginning of the *Annals* he says that he will present his history *sine ira et studio*, "without either bitterness or partiality." When a writer announces such a program at the commencement of his major works and boldly avows complete impartiality, it is only fair to ask how well has he accomplished his purpose. To many readers Tacitus appears to be anything but impartial or objective, and their answer then would be, "Not very well at all." But with Tacitus, as with all great historians, prejudice, if there be any, is part of his intellectual make-up, and one must ask the further question, "How did this come to be?" Indeed, another axiom, perhaps, of historical writing is that only men who believe deeply about their subject, whether with favor or disfavor, can write great history; and if that is the case, it is extremely difficult, nay impossible, to display objectivity such as could be anticipated from a computer.

As we have seen from the entire bulk of Tacitus's writing, it is clear that he became intrigued by the problem of the principate. As he grew older and more mature, he went ever farther back. The *Agricola*, his first attempt at historical writing, is only a make-piece before he will undertake the history of the present, the *beatissimum saeculum*. The *Agricola* is a contemporary work, concerned with a man of the previous and present generation. The *beatissimum saeculum* will be even more contemporary because it will go *pari passu* with the advance of Trajan's principate. The *Germany* and the *Dialogue* are similarly contemporary in focus although they do contain some flashes of historical probing. In the *Germany* are the history of the wars with the Germans over a span of 210 years and the prophetic statement of Rome's destiny in chapter thirty-three. In the *Dialogue* is the historical explanation for the decline of oratory in the present compared with that of the past. Nonetheless, both works are basically presentations of the present state—one concerned with a people, the other with an art.

When Tacitus had developed his historical tools in these short works, it would seem that the mid-point of Trajan's reign would have been the ideal time to undertake the history of the most happy age. But the event proved quite different. He rather went back to a point a bit more than a quarter of a century before the accession of Nerva, and then, with the completion of that large and great work, even further back, to describe the history of the Julio-Claudian period. In the third book of the *Annals* (24,3), he says that should he live long enough, he will write the history of the principate of Augustus. In other words Tacitus probed ever more deeply into the origins of the principate and, whereas, at the beginning of the *Annals*, he was concerned to speak of Augustus only as background to the accession of Tiberius, as he proceeded he evidently became dissatisfied with this starting point and realized that a history of the principate was meaningless without a close examination of the days of its founder.

Yet Tacitus must also have found that it was easier to write about the past than the present. Pliny and Juvenal, Suetonius and Plutarch felt the same way. All, with the likely exception of Juvenal, moved in the same circles and, if they did not know each other, at least had mutual friends. Pliny knew Tacitus and Suetonius, and may have known Plutarch, whose patron, Sosius Senecio, was a friend of his. Plutarch had friendly relations with numerous men of consular rank. On this important point the four are in accord. When one writes about current events, there is great danger of offense toward those still living; it is less dangerous, though still serious, to risk disfavor with the descendants of those who may be critically judged. Pliny and Juvenal clearly state that they desire to avoid such events; fear effectively blocks them. Pliny, further, does not wish to undertake the tedious labor necessary for the writing of history. But with Tacitus, although hesitation about discussing contemporary events and judging contemporary individuals may have some import, it plays a much less significant role; rather his passion about the past comes from his ever increasing philosophical inquiry and searching into the nature of the principate. Why did this come to pass? Is it only because Tacitus's historical sense became ever more refined and he was concerned with principle even more than with people? Was it perhaps disappointment, imperceptible at first but ever increasing, with Trajan who, in spite of being the best of emperors, the *optimus princeps*, left no doubt in the mind of a judicious observer that the Senate's role as an independent body in the government of empire was long since past? Though hailed so enthusiastically at the beginning of his reign, Trajan proves to be one of the strongest of emperors, perhaps against his will. It is one of the anomalies of the early history of the Roman Empire that power is most effectively consolidated in the hands of the best emperors, not the worst. They are not men who seek power to satisfy personal ambition, but they are respected and admired so enthusiastically and with such confidence that the people and the Senate both believe that the emperors can best perform the tasks that the empire required. Consequently, it is under Vespasian, Trajan, Hadrian, and Marcus Aurelius rather than under the principates of Caligula and Nero and Domitian that the increasing power of the emperor finds its firmest roots. Vis-à-vis the imperial power, the position of the senatorial order becomes increasingly more feeble. Tacitus, as one of the luminaries of this senatorial order, must have resented this although he fully realized that there was no other way.

Throughout his works, Tacitus is concerned not only with men but equally as much with the concepts of human behavior and human dignity. Among his great themes are *virtus*, "excellence"; *libertas*, "freedom"; *dignitas*, "personal honor";

and *capax imperii*, "capacity to rule." How do men meet their opportunities and their challenges? What is history's purpose? Tacitus said in the *Annals* (III:65,1) that the function of history is to record great achievements for emulation and despicable ones for eternal condemnation so that men will act knowing that posterity will judge them well or ill. But in the last analysis, although in the days of the republic there was chaos, there was yet opportunity for great men to flourish because of personal merit, while now in the empire the only truly great men can be the emperors and the members of their household. Opportunities for others are fewer and less grand. Nonetheless, a man will be judged by the manner in which he meets his challenges; and the emperors will be judged in accordance with the degree to which they allow the citizens of Rome, above all the members of the senatorial order, to have the opportunity to follow their own careers with the distinction appropriate to their ranks without danger and loss of integrity. For Tacitus does not believe that men are pre-destined and that they lack control over their own destiny. His views of *fortuna*, "fortune," and *fatum*, "fate," are in-consistent within his work; and it is difficult, if not impossible, to establish an unvarying philosophy of his thoughts on these important themes. On the whole men are responsible for their own actions. Although occasionally men may seem to be no more than the playthings of the gods, yet their intent and action often stand behind events. Tacitus expresses his thesis on this relationship in *Hist.* I:4,1: *ut non modo casus eventusque rerum, qui plerumque fortuiti sunt, sed ratio etiam causaeque noscantur*, "that so we may become acquainted, not only with the vicissitudes and the issues of events, which are often matters of chance, but also with their relation and their causes."

At the conclusion of the trial of Piso when, with his suicide, Germanicus's spirit and reputation could be considered paci-fied, a motion is made in the Senate that thanks be rendered to Tiberius, Augusta (Livia), Antonia, Agrippina, and Dru-sus. The name of Claudius was omitted; oversight or no, it was then added. Tacitus then muses on the mockery involved in human activity: *mihi, quanto plura recentium seu veterum revolvo, tanto magis ludibria rerum mortalium cunctis in negotiis obversantur. quippe fama spe veneratione potius omnes destinabantur imperio quam quem futurum principem fortuna in occulto tenebat (Ann.* III:18,4). "For my part, the wider the scope of my reflection on the present and the past, the more am I impressed by their mockery of human plans in every transaction. Clearly, the very last man marked out for empire by public opinion, expectation and general respect was he whom fortune was holding in reserve as the emperor of the future."

Marcus Lepidus receives high praise in the course of a senatorial debate and Tacitus wonders what it was in his case which enabled him to live a safe yet honorable life without compromising his integrity.

> *hunc ego Lepidum temporibus illis gravem et sapientem virum fuisse comperior: nam pleraque ab saevis adulationibus aliorum in melius flexit. neque tamen temperamenti egebat, cum aequabili auctoritate et gratia apud Tiberium viguerit. unde dubitare cogor, fato et sorte nascendi, ut cetera, ita principum inclinatio in hos, offensio in illos, an sit aliquid in nostris consiliis liceatque inter abruptam contumaciam et deforme obsequium pergere iter ambitione ac periculis vacuum (Ann.* IV:20,2–3).

This Lepidus, I am satisfied, was for that age a wise and high-principled man. Many a cruel suggestion made by the flattery of others he changed for the better, and yet he did not want tact, seeing that he always enjoyed an uniform prestige, and also the favour of Tiberius. This compels me to doubt whether the liking of princes for some men and their antipathy to others depend, like other contingencies, on a fate and destiny to which we are born, or, to some degree, on our own plans; so that it is possible to pursue a course between a defiant independence and a debasing servility, free from ambition and its perils.

In *Ann.* VI:22, Tacitus discourses upon astrology, destiny, and the relationship, if there is any, between gods and men. Tiberius was a keen student and devotee of the art and delighted in testing the skill of astrologers while strolling in his villa on Capri; those whom he found wanting were hurled to their death on the rocks below.

Sed mihi haec ac talia audienti in incerto iudicium est,
fatone res mortalium et necessitate immutabili an forte vol-
vantur. quippe sapientissimos veterum quique sectam eorum
aemulantur diversos reperies, ac multis insitam opinionem
non initia nostri, non finem, non denique homines dis curae;
ideo creberrime tristia in bonos, laeta apud deteriores esse.
contra alii fatum quidem congruere rebus putant, sed non e
vagis stellis, verum apud principia et nexus naturalium cau-
sarum; ac tamen electionem vitae nobis relinquunt, quam ubi
elegeris, certum imminentium ordinem. neque mala vel
bona, quae vulgus putet: multos, qui conflictari adversis vi-
deantur, beatos, at plerosque, quamquam magnas per opes,
miserrimos, si illi gravem fortunam constanter tolerent, hi
prospera inconsulte utantur. ceterum plurimis mortalium
non eximitur, quin primo cuiusque ortu ventura destinentur,
sed quaedam secus quam dicta sint cadere fallaciis ignara
dicentium: ita corrumpi fidem artis, cuius clara documenta et
antiqua aetas et nostra tulerit. quippe a filio eiusdem Thra-
sulli praedictum Neronis imperium in tempore memorabitur,
ne nunc incepto longius abierim.

When I hear of these and like occurrences, I suspend my
judgment on the question whether it is fate and unchange-
able necessity or chance which governs the revolutions of human affairs. Indeed, among the wisest of the ancients and
among their disciples you will find conflicting theories, many
holding the conviction that heaven does not concern itself
with the beginning or the end of our life, or, in short, with
mankind at all; and that therefore sorrows are continually
the lot of the good, happiness of the wicked; while others,
on the contrary, believe that, though there is a harmony between fate and events, yet it is not dependent on wandering
stars, but on primary elements, and on a combination of natural causes. Still, they leave us the capacity of choosing our
life, maintaining that, the choice once made, there is a fixed
sequence of events. Good and evil, again, are not what vulgar
opinion accounts them; many who seem to be struggling
with adversity are happy; many, amid great affluence, are
utterly miserable, if only the first bear their hard lot with
patience, and the latter make a foolish use of their prosperity.

Most men, however, cannot part with the belief that each
person's future is fixed from his very birth, but that some
things happen differently from what has been foretold
through the impostures of those who describe what they do

not know, and that this destroys the credit of a science, clear testimonies to which have been given both by past ages and by our own. In fact, how the son of this same Thrasyllus predicted Nero's reign I shall relate when the time comes, not to digress too far from my subject.

Whatever the impact of the gods and fate, that men are on the whole their own masters seems clear. As Corbulo lamented, it was not possible for him to have the same opportunities for greatness as his predecessors in the republic had had. Nonetheless, he reached heights of prestige and power that were unmatched by any general of the early principate. His career could be considered parallel to those of Pompey the Great or of Lucullus.

It is when men are crushed in their opportunity to fulfill their *dignitas* and display their *virtus* that Tacitus's anger is vividly displayed. He himself describes such circumstances, which followed upon the death of Agricola, and his view is corroborated by Pliny the Younger.

> He has as considerable compensation for his hastened death the fact that he escaped that last period, in which Domitian drained the state, no longer at intervals and with respites of time, but with, as it were, one continuous blow. Agricola did not see the senate-house under siege and the senate ringed by arms and, in one and the same massacre, the murders of so many men of consular rank, the exiles and flights of so many very distinguished women. Mettius Carus was credited with only one triumph, Messalinus' violent opinion had influence only within the citadel at Alba, and Baebius Massa was already then a defendant: soon our hands led Helvidius to prison; the sight of Mauricus and Rusticus dishonored us, and Senecio drenched us with guiltless blood. Nero at least withdrew his eyes and ordered his crimes but did not watch them: an especial part of misery under Domitian was to see and to be seen, when our sighs were noted down, when that savage face and ruddy expression, with which he fortified himself against shame, were able to mark out the paleness of so many men (*Agr.* 44,5–45,2).
>
> Though this is the place where recently that fearful monster built his defences with untold terrors, where lurking in his den he licked up the blood of his murdered relatives or

emerged to plot the massacre and destruction of his most distinguished subjects. Menaces and horror were the sentinels at his doors, and the fears alike of admission and rejection; then himself in person, dreadful to see and to meet, with arrogance on his brow and fury in his eye, a womanish pallor over his body but a deep flush to match the shameless expression on his face. None dared approach him, none dared speak; always he sought darkness and mystery, and only emerged from the desert of his solitude to create another (*Panegyricus* 48,3–5).

Here perhaps is the source of Tacitus's dissatisfaction with the principate after the first years of Trajan as exemplified by the increasing disillusion of the *Annals*. Though there were about a dozen men who reached second consulates under Trajan (only two gained a third) and the emperor seemed not to fear the rivalry of a potential challenge from among his subordinates, yet the opportunity for senators to satisfy their *dignitas* depended totally upon imperial good will.

But another question rises. How much of this is conscious? The truest answer may be, none. Tacitus's feelings are ingrained in his mind and his emotions; and as he looks back over the history of the principate before Trajan, he focuses most particularly upon Tiberius because, with the accession of Tiberius, the principate became a continuing form of government. Before that it might have been considered no more than another of the aberrations away from the senatorial form of government as exemplified in the first chapter of the *Annals*. In the *Annals* he is, among other things, concerned with the baneful effects of the principate's powers upon the character of the rulers; and he writes of the gradual disintegration of Tiberius with the bitter memories of Domitian foremost in his mind. Yet he is not being intentionally fraudulent; there is no instance of factual error in his works that can be ascribed to ulterior motives. In fact, most of the material available for rehabilitation of Tiberius's reputation in modern times comes from Tacitus's pages. The facts, good and bad, are presented with accuracy and without distortion; the emphasis placed upon good and bad varies greatly. For Tacitus is concerned with more than a bare recitation of facts. It is in his probing of the depths of the human mind that his interpretation of the motives of the individual is colored by his remembrance of things past. It is here that his powers of suggestion, his skill in innuendo, weigh so heavily; he is masterful in presenting evidence on both sides of a question so that the view that he wishes remembered will be presented last and at greater length than the opposing one, as we have seen above. The view favored is invariably the one which will do the greatest harm to the individual involved.

Is Tacitus therefore to be denied the title of historian? In a scientific age it is a commonplace that history should, and must, be "objective." But it may perhaps reasonably be asked, has there ever been an "objective" historian? We must insist upon scrupulous treatment of facts; but facts must always be interpreted, judgments must be made, suggestions concerning motives must be advanced. And these interpretations, judgments, and suggestions are made by human beings who are molded by their own experiences. History is not written in a vacuum nor by machines; it is written by fallible individuals, no two of whom will likely agree on every facet of a series of events. In our own days we need recall no more than the varying judgments of Adolf Hitler that have issued forth in England and the United States; if one assumes that all students of Hitler have the same basic stock of material upon which to draw, one often wonders how judgments so disparate can be drawn from them.

So it was with Tacitus. A child of his age, as are all human beings to a greater or lesser degree, his outlook was conditioned by his personal experience and, as he grew older, he began to realize that the reconciliation which he had hailed in 98 was an actual impossibility. For he became aware of the fundamental problem of the principate, which is that of deceit. Beginning with Augustus's first settlement after the battle of Actium in 31 B.C., effective control of the empire was in the hands of the emperor, who was commander-in-chief of the army and had tremendous financial resources at his disposal, as well as the unique prestige that his position helped bestow upon him. The *respublica restituta*, the restored republic of which Augustus boasted in the record of his achievements that he composed late in life, the *Res gestae*, could not actually exist; for the seat of effective power had shifted from the

Senate to the emperor. Yet, for the sake of appearance and the morale of the senatorial order, it must seem to exist; this could not be accomplished without deception or fraud. Whether the new form of government was good or bad, whether Augustus himself was an idealistic ruler or a self-seeking power politician are questions that need not be discussed here. But it is certain that they are questions that Tacitus considered in the maturity of years, and the *Annals* give us his answers. And it is likewise certain that his penetrating insight into the interrelationships of men and events has rarely, if ever, been surpassed; generations that have witnessed great heights of power politics and the reigns of vicious tyrants can still find many pertinent judgments in Tacitus's pages. It used to be said that Tacitus painted individuals worse than they could possibly be; the twentieth century has learned to know how ruthless and morally degraded men can become under pressure.

The information that Tacitus presents is almost invariably accurate. He has, in many instances, been supported by the discoveries of archaeology, by epigraphical evidence, and by other authors. The handling of material is his own, but what he offers is beyond reproach. No historian of antiquity can have more demanded of him.

In Tacitus's writing, his personal judgments of men and events play an important role. They are interwoven with the description of what men did and what events occurred so that his subjective judgments intrude upon objective narrative. Tacitus is trying to show that the principate will destroy men, not only those subordinate to the emperor but the emperor himself; his personal view is put into the mouth of Lucius Arruntius late in the sixth book. If Tiberius had not been able to withstand the crushing burden of empire, what hope from Gaius?

Tacitus writes not only as a historian but as a psychologist and a dramatist. The interplay of human motive and the attempt to present actions in the grand tradition of Greek tragedy are always present. The reader must be alert to try to understand Tacitus fully, alert not only to his historical purpose and to the means whereby he accomplished it, but also to his failings, most particularly perhaps in his presentation of character as unchanging. Tacitus is not unique in this among the ancients. A belief that a man was born with all his traits fully developed was widespread. Therefore, if characteristics do not appear for many years, the reason is not that they were at first absent and only gradually appeared, but that they were skillfully concealed. Hence, deception is always necessary. Tacitus's presentation of Tiberius especially would have been very different had he known what psychologists now know; and the gradual degeneration, as it were the revelation, layer by layer, of Tiberius's true nature, might not have appeared at all.

When Tacitus presents a judgment on people and events, it is one in which he honestly believes. He believes that these individuals, these details, these events will fit into the grand panorama of the principate that he is painting. We may differ in our interpretation of detail, we may challenge him on conclusions, but we have no right to say that he is absolutely wrong and that he lied; for he believed that what he was writing was being written *sine ira et studio*. The modern reader will surely have to grant that Tacitus's work, like Churchill's *History of the Second World War*, is personal to a degree that few histories have reached; he may disagree with Tacitus on points of interpretation, but he should not deny him recognition of historical integrity.

X. SURVIVAL AND
POPULARITY

Pliny's prophecy, concerning which he had been so confident, proved to be idle. Whatever the reason, Tacitus's historical work was anything but popular in the years after his death and, indeed, at any time in antiquity. Conjecture can attempt to explain why. There is no question but that Tacitus's Latin is hard and difficult to understand; even Romans must have found it exercising. Further, there was a change in the intellectual climate of the day. Historical analysis was a difficult enterprise; biography furnished information as well as amusement; and two of Tacitus's contemporaries, Suetonius and Plutarch, foreshadowed the trend of historical studies for several centuries to come. The accession of the emperor Hadrian, with his predilection for things archaic, exemplified by his preference for Cato over Livy, must have put obstacles in the path of Tacitus's acceptance. This is particularly so since his style, although it is not a continuation of the extravagances found in Seneca, is far more rhetorical and far more carefully wrought than an archaizing age would care to tolerate. And, from another point of view, if it is true that Tacitus's deep concern for and criticism of Tiberius look toward contemporary events at the beginning of Hadrian's reign and intentionally recall that emperor's personality, then one would expect that acceptance during that period of some twenty years would hardly be widespread.

Throughout the remainder of classical antiquity, there are only scattered references to Tacitus's works. Some are valuable because they allude to or give us information about parts of his work that are now lost. But all in all, they are a very mixed bag. There are many instances where one may assume that an author was familiar with Tacitus, but there is no evidence to prove it.

Around the beginning of the third century the Christian Tertullian, in his bitter and enthusiastic *Apologeticus*, cites Tacitus in the most unflattering terms regarding the history of the Jews. He refers to the fifth book of the *Histories* and comments that Tacitus was totally wrong in claiming that the Jews worshipped an ass's head. He calls Tacitus *ille mendaciorum loquacissimus*, "that famous man who is full of lies," which may involve a play of words upon Tacitus's name which, of course, means "The Silent One." The *Historia Augusta*, the collection of imperial biographies which continued those of Suetonius and which purported to be the work of six separate authors written in the days of Diocletian and Constantine, is now generally recognized as the product of one author who fraudulently represented himself as a committee and who wrote toward the end of the fourth century. There are three references to Tacitus in this collection, all in lives purportedly written by Flavius Vopiscus. The most important is in the life of the emperor Tacitus, who reigned for a period of six months in the year 275; he claimed to be a descendant of the historian and, since he was dismayed that his works were almost totally unavailable, he arranged to have ten copies produced at public expense annually and placed in public libraries. Since his reign was so brief, the effect of this policy if, indeed, it did exist, could not have been very great. Further references in the lives of Aurelian and Probus indicate that Tacitus's reputation was not high. He was considered an artist, but he was not reliable because he was not truthful. These citations, however, show little more than that his name was known, for the *Vita Taciti* is almost totally fictitious, and the reference to his mendacity in the *Vita Aureliani* is a joke.

The great historian Ammianus Marcellinus, who was probably a contemporary if not a model (in a perverse way) for the writer of the *Historia Augusta*, reveals kinship with Tacitus. There are a few passages which show that Ammianus knew Tacitus, but beyond that there is emulation of the general tone and the effects which are sought. Further, his own history, originally spanning thirty-one books, covers the period from the death of Domitian to the fateful year of 378 in his own day. Tacitus's *Histories*, as we know, ended with Domitian's assassination in 96. Ammianus thus boldly claims to be Tacitus's successor.

Sulpicius Severus in the early fifth century cites Tacitus's *Histories* in connection with Christianity. The great church father Jerome records that Tacitus's historical work, the *Histories* and the *Annals*, spanned thirty books. In the fifth century Sidonius Apollinaris, an exemplar of a modest Gallic renaissance, mentions Tacitus as a historian less great than one of his own friends. Orosius, the student and follower of St. Augustine who published a history entitled *Against the Pagans* in 417, in reaction to the charges made against Christianity as having been responsible for the sack of Rome by the Goths in 410, cites several passages from Tacitus. They are all from the *Histories* and, of course, it is here where Tacitus is most concerned with the affairs of the East, the lands that are to us the Holy Lands. Orosius is not an original writer, but he was a careful compiler and the information that he gives us can be considered reliable; his use of Tacitus shows that the historian's text was available to one who sought in the first quarter of the fifth century.

From this point on there is practically nothing for a span of almost three centuries. Indeed, from 650 to 850 the age is totally dark. Then there is evidence that Tacitus survives and is read in the great religious community of Fulda in Germany. And it is in Fulda and in nearby cities such as Hersfeld that much of Tacitus's heritage is preserved. Thereupon until the eleventh century, again very little is known. The manuscripts that survive, though few in number, can largely be dated to this period, indicating a revival of interest in the historian. In Monte Cassino, for example, Peter the Deacon read the *Agricola* around 1135 and paraphrased some of its material in his own work. The next important steps, however, come with the discovery, as it were, of his works; and the first impact of Tacitus upon the Renaissance is linked with the great figure of Boccaccio. Boccaccio knew and read the manuscript known as the Second Medicean, which contains *Annals* XI through XVI and *Histories* I through V, although in the manuscript they are numbered consecutively XI through XXI. Boccaccio was able somehow, perhaps even dishonestly, to remove this manuscript from the library of Monte Cassino around 1360, and it thereby became known to a wider world. He was not, however, the first one to read it. It had been read and digested some twenty years before in the 1340s. But it is Boccaccio, nonetheless, who introduces Tacitus to the Italian Renaissance. Petrarch, his greater predecessor, did not know Tacitus. The minor works derive from a manuscript from Hersfeld which was brought to Italy about the year 1455 by a monk, Enoch of Ascoli. It was evidently known to Italians about a quarter of a century earlier; once it arrived in Italy, knowledge of it became fairly widespread. Poggio Bracciolini, the renowned discoverer of so many ancient manuscripts in the early fifteenth century, also played an important role in Tacitus's revival. The *editio princeps* of Tacitus, which appeared about 1470, included the material of the Second Medicean and the Hersfeldensis. It was not until 1509 that the First Medicean, which contains the first six books of the *Annals*, became known; the first printed edition which included these books appeared in 1515.

The history of Tacitus's impact upon thought in the West is a checkered one. There are periods in which he is valued in his own right; there are others in which his importance stems from the fact that he can be interpreted symbolically, one way or another, to represent thoughts that have been at that time proscribed. He is a natural match for Machiavelli, although Machiavelli did not know the Tiberius books and referred little to the remainder of Tacitus's work. When Machiavelli was put on the Index late in the sixteenth century, Tacitus served as his substitute, interpreted by many as an outspoken opponent of monarchy and absolutism. Yet one of the oddities of the reading of Tacitus is that he is a handbook for both monarchists and antimonarchists. He shows how good men can live under regimes which are dangerous and destructive of human capacity and also how terrible tyranny can be both for the ruler and for his subjects. His impact was particularly strong in Italy and the Low Countries (the latter because of their violent religious and political opposition to Spain) where he became a symbol of the opposition to tyranny.

The high point of Tacitus's influence was the century from 1580 to 1680, the age of the Baroque, and it may be that the enthusiasm for exuberance and rococo typified by this type of architecture and sculpture was engendered also by the virtuosity of Tacitus's prose. The number of editions of his works that was produced in this period is unparalleled in the history of the survival of Tacitus. He was studied, lectured upon, edited, and explained by many of the most renowned scholars and public figures of the day, chiefly the great Justus Lipsius in Holland and Marc Antoine Muret in Italy. Then there is a very severe slackening in interest. As the intellectual and political climate of Europe changed, Tacitus's importance waned. His popularity declined markedly, particularly with the ruling classes, and Napoleon perhaps best exemplified the disdain of rulers for the historian. He said on separate occasions, *Tacite . . . calomnie l'Empire* ("Tacitus insults the Empire,") and *Tacite! Ne me parlez pas de ce pamphlétaire. Il a calomnié les empereurs* ("Don't speak to me of that pamphleteer. He has insulted the emperors"). Further, he described Tacitus as a *détracteur de l'humanité* ("a detractor of humanity"). Here is one of the major examples of the criticism that Tacitus describes people as being worse than they are.

In the nineteenth century and the first half of the twentieth this valuation of Tacitus remained general. His stature among Roman historians was generally low. Livy was normally given prime position, with Sallust a worthy second. But in recent years, particularly since World War II, Tacitus has risen greatly in favor; and his impact, his power, his abilities, and judgments are appreciated as in no other period since the heights of *Tacitism*, the age of the Baroque. It is now clear that the world in which we live is not the best of all possible worlds, and the concept of progress and improvement which was one of the main undercurrents of nineteenth century thought has long been out of favor. The world is irrational; men are often mad. And since this is the case, the historian of a comparable world, similarly out of joint and peopled by high and low alike who are evil or ineffective, cannot fail to have a contemporary significance.

We are currently in the second great revival of Tacitus. He is in this day among the most widely read and studied Latin authors. Tacitus would have been amused, were the dead able to have knowledge in an afterlife, to see that his great impact had been delayed for so many centuries and that it was in a world which, like his own, was undergoing and had undergone violent change that he was considered, not a prophet of the future, but one of the most brilliant of all interpreters of the past.

Yet it is sobering to realize how narrow the thread of survival was in his case. For many authors, Vergil and Horace particularly, there are numerous manuscripts, many of them of great antiquity; and their texts are consequently very sound. Other authors are not similarly fortunate in either antiquity or number of manuscripts. Nonetheless, it is often possible for skillful editors to reconstruct a close approximation of the original text. But with Tacitus's major works there was one manuscript for the first six books of the *Annals*, another for the combined last six books of the *Annals* and the surviving five of the *Histories*. I say this knowing full well that there are scholars who argue that another manuscript, Leidensis, is independent of the Second Medicean for the tradition of these eleven books. My own view is that it is not, and therefore each half of the great works comes to us from only one manuscript.

The survival of the minor works was only slightly more secure because the existing manuscripts derive from one, Hersfeldensis. Only Catullus among major Latin authors survives by as slender a thread. It is saddening to realize how great the loss would have been in the study of Latin antiquity had those single manuscripts not survived the ages and been discovered. We, their posterity, would be totally unaware of the genius of these two innovators in Latin poetry and prose, both of them provincial in the old sense and symbolic of the expansion of the power and influence of the Roman Empire. The Roman State profited from the transfusion of genius stemming from the north of Italy and the south of Gaul. Rome did indeed absorb the best abilities of all peoples in the process of transforming a world into a city.

SELECTED
BIBLIOGRAPHY

The items that follow are, with one exception, all in English. That exception is the new article by Borzsák in the great German classical encyclopedia. For surveys of recent work in the field and a discussion of the present state of Tacitean studies, see F. R. D. Goodyear, *Tacitus* (*Greece and Rome: New Surveys in the Classics.* No. 4, 1970); H. W. Benario, "Recent Work on Tacitus (1954–1963)," *Classical World*, 58 (1964–1965): 69–83, and "Recent Work on Tacitus (1964–1968)," *Classical World*, 63 (1969–1970): 253–267; and the bibliography in R. Syme, *Tacitus.*

Africa, T. W. "The Historian—Tacitus," in *Rome of the Caesars.* New York: Wiley, 1965. Pp. 157–170.

Beare, W. "Tacitus on the Germans," *Greece and Rome,* 11 (1964): 64–76.

Borzsák, S. "P. Cornelius Tacitus," in Pauly–Wissowa, *Realencylopädie der classischen Altertumswissenschaft,* Suppl. 11. Stuttgart: Alfred Druckenmüller, 1968. Cols. 373–512. Also issued separately.

Burke, P. "Tacitism," in *Tacitus* (*Studies in Latin Literature and Its Influence*). Edited by T. A. Dorey. London: Routledge & Kegan Paul, 1969. Pp. 149–171.

Dudley, D. R. *The World of Tacitus.* Boston: Little, Brown, 1968.

Laistner, M. L. W. "Tacitus and His Forerunners" and "Tacitus, the Historian," in *The Greater Roman Historians.* Berkeley and

Los Angeles: University of California Press, 1947. Pp. 103–140.

Löfstedt, E. "On the Style of Tacitus," *Journal of Roman Studies*, 38 (1948): 1–8; a longer version appears in *Roman Literary Portraits* (Oxford: Clarendon Press, 1958), pp. 157–180, under the title "The Style of Tacitus."

Martin, R. H. "Tacitus and His Predecessors," in Dorey, *Tacitus*, pp. 117–147.

Mendell, C. W. *Tacitus: The Man and His Work*. New Haven: Yale University Press, 1957.

Miller, N. P. "Style and Content in Tacitus," in Dorey, *Tacitus*, pp. 99–116.

Otis, B. "The Uniqueness of Latin Literature," *Arion*, 6 (1967): 185–206.

Quinn, K. "Tacitus' Narrative Technique," in *Latin Explorations: Critical Studies in Roman Literature*. London: Routledge & Kegan Paul, 1963. Pp. 110–129.

Ryberg, I. S. "Tacitus' Art of Innuendo," *Transactions and Proceedings of the American Philological Association*, 73 (1942): 383–404.

Syme, R. *Tacitus*. 2 vols. Oxford: Clarendon Press, 1958.

Syme, R. "The Political Opinions of Tacitus," in *Ten Studies in Tacitus*. Oxford: Clarendon Press, 1970. Pp. 119–140.

von Fritz, K. "Tacitus, Agricola, Domitian, and the Problem of the Principate," *Classical Philology*, 52 (1957): 73–97.

Walker, B. *The Annals of Tacitus: A Study in the Writing of History*. Manchester: Manchester University Press, 1952.

Wellesley, K. "Tacitus as a Military Historian," in Dorey, *Tacitus*, pp. 63–97.

INDEX

This index contains all proper names, with the exception of Tacitus, Rome, Romans, Italy, and Italians, some Latin expressions, and a few other items. The names are listed according to their most common forms; there is thus an inconsistency, since some will be listed by the *nomen* and others by the *cognomen*. If an individual is not found under one part of his name, the reader should check the other. Full names have been given for every person listed, as far as these are known, with occasional further distinguishing characteristics to avoid confusion among similar names.

Generic names are listed and include all references to adjectival and other forms; *Germany*, for example, includes *German, Germans,* and *Germanic.*

Ammianus Marcellinus, 161
Anauni, 69
Ancus Marcius, 102
Angrivarii, 63
Anicetus, 72, 74, 75
Annals, 12, 43, 46, 57–79, 80–93
    passim, 112, 117, 120, 124,
    129–36 passim, 139, 146–52
    passim, 155, 157, 161, 162, 164
Antistius Vetus, Gaius, 93, 94
Antium, 72
Antonia (mother of Germanicus
    and Claudius), 151
Antonius, Marcus, 7, 8, 96–99 pas-
    sim, 127
Antonius Primus, Marcus, 51, 111,
    112, 122
Apennines, 2
Aper, Marcus, 40, 42, 82, 89, 108
Apicius, Marcus Gavius, 93, 94
Apologeticus, 160
Apulia, 2
Aquitania, 13, 22
Arabia Nabataea, 58
Arausio, 32
Arcanus, 90, 91, 134, 135, 136
Ariovistus, 54
Armenia, 118, 140
Arminius, 32, 62, 86
Arruntius, Lucius, 68, 157
Arsaces, 37
Artabanus, 138
Arulenus Rusticus, Quintus Junius,
    26
Asia, 14, 15, 22, 23, 29, 69, 125,
    135, 138
Asinius Agrippa, Marcus (cos. 25,
    son of Gallus), 126
Asinius Gallus, Gaius (cos. 8 B.C.,
    son of Pollio), 116
Asinius Pollio, Gaius (cos. 40
    B.C.), 21, 126
Asinius Pollio, Gaius (cos. 23, son
    of Gallus), 93, 94
Asylum, 52
Athens, 64, 101
Aufidius Bassus, 82
Augusta. *See* Livia
Augustine, 161
Augustus, 9, 10, 11, 32, 33, 37, 43,
    44, 49, 53, 56–67 passim, 80,
    91–100 passim, 103, 112, 113,
    115, 121, 126, 127, 128, 134,
    135, 136, 139, 143, 144, 146,
    149, 156, 157
Aurelian, 160

Baebius Massa, 18, 154
Baiae, 72, 73
Balbi, 101
Barea Soranus, Quintus Marcius,
    140
Baroque, 163
Batavi, 54
Bauli, 73
Bedriacum, 48, 110, 111
Bibaculus, Marcus Furius, 127
Bithynia, 15
Blaesus, Junius, 130
Boccaccio, 162
Boudicca, 118, 120
Britain, 13, 22, 23, 28, 45, 55, 64,
    84, 92, 117, 118, 119, 120, 139,
    142
Britannicus, 69, 72, 140
Bructeri, 32
Brundisium, 9, 97, 98
Brutus, Lucius Junius, 1
Brutus, Marcus Junius, 7, 8, 97, 98,
    126, 127
Brutus Albinus, Decimus Junius,
    97, 98
Burrus, Sextus Afranius, 69, 74,
    115, 136

Caecina Alienus, Aulus, 48, 50,
    111
Caelian, 76
Caelius Vivenna, 103
Caepio, Quintus Servilius, 37
Caesar, Gaius Julius (the deified
    Julius), 7, 8, 9, 10, 37, 104,
    112, 126, 127
Caesar, Gaius, 66, 67, 93, 94
Caesar, Lucius, 66, 67
Caesar (Germanicus), 63
Caesar (Tiberius), 137
Caesar Octavianus, 97, 98. *See also*
    Octavius, Gaius (Octavianus)
Caesars, 48, 74, 97, 99, 118, 127
Caledonia, 92
Calgacus, 23, 28, 54, 128, 141
Caligula. *See* Gaius
Camerium, 101
Campania, 45, 66
Cannae, 2, 32, 54
Capax imperii, 61, 91, 118, 121,
    130, 144, 151
Capitol (Capitoline), 45, 51, 52,
    77, 109
Capri, 66, 152
Carbo, Gnaeus Papirius, 37
Carthage, 4, 32, 37, 123

Livy (Titus Livius), 21, 34, 79, 80, 81, 86, 89, 105, 126, 159, 163
Locusta, 140
Lollius, Marcus, 97, 99
Low Countries, 163
Lucan (Marcus Annaeus Lucanus), 24, 89
Lucania, 101
Lucrine, lake, 74
Lucullus, Lucius Licinius, 118, 154
Lyons, 69, 101, 104

Machiavelli, 162
Macro, Quintus Naevius Cordus Sutorius, 68
Maecenas, Gaius, 78, 79, 129
Maiestas: treason, 62, 122, 126; dignity of language, 88
Marcellus, Gaius Claudius, 66, 67, 136
Marcellus, Titus Clodius Eprius, 120
Marcus Aurelius, 33, 145, 150
Marius, Gaius, 6, 37, 92, 93, 96, 97, 124, 131
Martialis, Cornelius, 51
Martin, R. H., 145
Mastarna, 103
Maternus, Curiatius, 39–42 passim, 108, 145, 146
Mauretania, 118
Mauricus, Junius, 154
Maximus, 19
Maximus, Gnaeus Mallius, 37
Medicean, First, 162
Medicean, Second, 162, 164
Mediterranean, 2, 3, 4
Meherdates, 138
Mela, Pomponius, 84
Memoirs (of Agrippina and Corbulo), 84
Messala Corvinus, Marcus Valerius, 126
Messalina, Valeria, 114
Messalinus, Lucius Valerius Catullus, 154
Messalla, Vipstanus, 40, 41, 83, 85
Metelli, 6
Metellus Caprarius, Gaius Caecilius, 37
Mettius Carus, 154
Minerva, 72
Minicius Fundanus, Gaius, 19
Misenum, 72, 73
Mons Graupius, 28, 29, 92, 117
Monte Cassino, 161, 162

Mucianus, Gaius Licinius, 47–51 passim, 108, 112, 117, 119, 120, 146
Muret, Marc Antoine, 163

Napoleon, 163
Narbon Gaul. *See* Gallia Narbonensis
Narcissus, Tiberius Claudius, 114
Nero, 10, 12, 14, 43–53 passim, 58, 69–79 passim, 83, 84, 111, 115, 116, 117, 119, 125, 130, 133–45 passim, 150, 153, 154
Nero (Tiberius), 37
Nero (father of Tiberius), 66, 67, 97, 99
Nerva, 10–14 passim, 26, 27, 36, 46, 119, 128, 129, 142, 144, 145, 149
Nola, 96, 97
Norbanus, Gaius, 53
Numa Pompilius, 102
Numidia, 92

Obaritus, 75
Ocresia, 102
Octavia, 69, 71
Octavius, Gaius (Octavianus), 7, 8, 9, 53, 59, 61, 100
Octavius, Gaius (father of Augustus), 96, 97
Ollius, Titus, 114, 115
Optimus princeps, 11, 144, 150
Orosius, 161
Otho, 10, 48, 50, 71, 85, 110, 111, 114, 118, 119, 120, 131, 132, 133, 143, 144

Pacorus, 37
Palatine, 76, 109
Pallas, 72, 114, 140
Panegyricus, 15, 18, 154–55
Pannonia, 62, 113
Pansa Caetronianus, Gaius Vibius, 97, 98, 100
Parthia, 32, 37, 45, 58, 64, 78, 138
Peloponnesian War, 3
Pericles, 101
Persicus, 104
Peter the Deacon, 161
Petrarch, 162
Petronius (perhaps Titus Petronius Niger), 119
Pharsalia, 24
Pharsalus (Pharsalia), 7, 131
Philippi, 8, 127, 131
Pinarius Natta, 126

Piso, Gaius Calpurnius (leader of the conspiracy), 125, 139
Piso, Gnaeus Calpurnius (rival of Germanicus), 64, 113, 151
Piso Frugi Licinianus, Lucius Calpurnius (designated successor of Galba), 143, 144
Placentia, 111
Plato, 129
Plinius Caecilius Secundus, Gaius (Pliny the Younger), 13–21 passim, 24, 30, 39, 44, 83, 84, 88, 90, 121, 149, 150, 154, 159
Plinius Secundus, Gaius (Pliny the Elder), 12, 18, 31, 83, 84, 86
Plotius Firmus, 110
Plutarch (Lucius Mestrius Plutarchus), 85, 149, 159
Po, 101
Poggio Bracciolini, 162
Pollio. *See* Asinius
Polybius, 3, 4, 21, 54, 123
Pompeianus (referring to Livy), 126
Pompeius Magnus, Gnaeus, 6, 7, 9, 118, 124, 126, 131, 154
Pompeius Magnus Pius, Sextus, 97, 98
Pontius Pilatus, 77
Poppaea Sabina, 71, 114, 115, 121
Poppaeus Sabinus, Gaius, 114, 115
Porcii, 101, 105
Porsenna, Lars, 52
Potentia, 129–36 passim
Praetorian guard, 13, 47, 65, 69, 74, 93, 94, 110, 111, 129, 144
Priam, 109
Princeps/principatus, 9, 91, 127–41 passim, 147
Priscus, Marius, 14, 16, 18, 19, 39
Probus, 160
Proserpina, 77
Ptolemy, 7
Punic Wars, 2, 3, 4
Pyrrhus, 4

Quintilianus, Marcus Fabius, 38, 39, 79, 81, 82, 88, 89

Red Sea, 58
Renaissance, 162
Res gestae, 99, 100, 156
Rex/regnum, 91, 127–140 passim
Rhine, 31, 32, 33, 37, 54, 142
Rhodes, 66, 67

Roman History of Velleius Paterculus, 81
Romulus, 1, 101, 102, 105
Rubrum mare, 57, 58
Rusticus, Quintus Junius Arulenus, 154
Rutilius Rufus, Publius, 26

Sabines, 52, 56, 102
Sallustius, Gaius, 4, 21, 44, 65, 78–81 passim, 88, 92–96 passim, 123, 124, 137, 138, 163
Sallustius Crispus, Gaius, 60, 78, 91, 129, 134
Samnites, 32, 37, 102
Sarmatae, 45
Satrius Secundus, 126
Saturn, 133
Saturninus, Lucius Appuleius, 124
Scaurus, Marcus Aemilius (princeps senatus), 26
Scaurus, Marcus Aemilius (legate of Mallius Maximus), 37
Scipio, Quintus Caecilius Metellus Pius, 126
Scipio Aemilianus Africanus, Publius Cornelius, 123
Scipio Africanus, Publius Cornelius, 5
Scipio Asiaticus, Lucius Cornelius, 53
Scipios, 7
Scotland, 28, 142
"Second Sophistic," 87
Secundus, Julius, 40, 41
Sejanus, Lucius Aelius, 65–68 passim, 81, 82, 85, 93–96 passim, 111–15 passim, 121, 126, 130, 135, 137, 139
Seneca, Lucius Annaeus, 69, 70, 71, 74, 83, 89, 115, 116, 121, 136, 159
Senecio, Herennius, 26, 154
Senones, 102
Servilius Nonianus, Marcus, 82
Servius Tullius, 53, 102
Shakespeare, 8
Sibylline books, 12, 77
Sidonius Apollinaris, 161
Silanus, Marcus Junius, 69, 115, 135, 138
Sinus Arabicus, 58
Sosius Senecio, Quintus, 149
Spain, 5, 37, 101, 110, 117, 163
Sparta, 101
Spelunca, 66, 114
Sperlonga, 66

INDEX OF PASSAGES IN TACITUS